BUSINESS OF FASHION

FIONA PAULSON. T

AF670227

Copyright © Fiona Paulson. T
All Rights Reserved.

This book has been published with all efforts taken to make the material error-free after the consent of the author. However, the author and the publisher do not assume and hereby disclaim any liability to any party for any loss, damage, or disruption caused by errors or omissions, whether such errors or omissions result from negligence, accident, or any other cause.

While every effort has been made to avoid any mistake or omission, this publication is being sold on the condition and understanding that neither the author nor the publishers or printers would be liable in any manner to any person by reason of any mistake or omission in this publication or for any action taken or omitted to be taken or advice rendered or accepted on the basis of this work. For any defect in printing or binding the publishers will be liable only to replace the defective copy by another copy of this work then available.

I dedicate this book to all young budding Designers who are starting their step into the feild of Fashion and also to all those who supported me to write this book

Contents

Foreword

My whole carrier has been dedicated to pursue the vision of Fashion. I decided I wanted to give the business world an idea about Fashion business. The Business of Fashion's core mission is to open, inform and connect the global fashion industry, Fasion students, young budding fashion enthusiastics . At the core of this mission is their dedication to creating, curating and distributing high-quality news and analysis. They do so with complete editorial independence, free from investor influence, commercial pressures or personal bias.

That's about the time i discovered the importance and The Business of fashion book came into vision.

Preface

Its been a long time coming, but Business and exposure with fashion opens a wide global outpouring change, exposing ones mind with the idea of fashion was the insidious element of publication.

Business of Fashion dealing with style in clothes, cosmetics, behaviour, etc, esp the latest or most admired style, focuses primarily on the design, manufacturing, merchandising, branding, marketing & retailing across all aspects of the business of fashion. Business of Fashion plays a directional and supporting role in the evolution of branded fashion around the world.This book is a strategic and market oriented blend of the main perspectives in fashion business; covering strategy, budgeting, finance, prodcut development, fashion marketing, communication, branding, retail operations management and global distribution channels. Fashion has the ability to change and shape lives through its personal connection to us all. We all have to wear clothes and every piece of clothing we buy represents a personal choice – it is this intrinsically human relationship between us and our fashion that makes it political.

Acknowledgements

WRITING A BOOK IS MORE HARDER THAN I THOUGHT AND more rewarding than I could ever imagined. none of this would have been possible without my Mother Biji Paulson. She was the first person i made when i moved during my struggles. She understood my struggles and stood by me with all my sucesses.

I'm eternal glad to my Institution and my fellow friends who encouraged me during my writing , staffs of Departent of Costume Design for their help and support to carry out this work.

I would like to thank the Almighty God for its supreme power, without which this work would not have completed successfully.

Prologue

Congratulation!, the fact that you're reading this means you've taken one step closer to know more about Fashion and its idea in Business. Do not put this book down, let this give you more idea for your carrier and develop your passion for Fashion and Fashion Business.

CHAPTER I

WORLD OF FASHION-An overview

AIMS AND OBJECTIVES

The Business of Fashion is an online magazine and website dedicated to the world of fashion. It was founded in 2007 by Imran Amed and has gained a global following as an essential daily resource for fashion creatives, executives and entrepreneurs in over 200 countries. It is frequently described as "indispensable," "required reading" and "an addiction."

1. Understanding the fashion business
2. Discuss about the fashion business
3. Discuss about the business size and structure
4. Understanding the business environment
5. Understanding the business current trend

INTRODUCTION

The Business of Fashion was founded in 2007 by Imran Amed, a fashion business advisor, writer and digital entrepreneur; *The Business of Fashion* began as a project of passion, aiming to fill the void for an informed, analytical and opinionated point of view on the fashion business.

MEANING OF BUSINESS IN FASHION

Prior to the mid-19th century, most clothing was custom-made. It was handmade for individuals, either as home production or on order from dressmakers and tailors. By the beginning of the 20th century-with the rise of new technologies such as the sewing machine, the rise of global capitalism and the development of the factory system of production, and the proliferation of retail outlets such as department stores-clothing had increasingly come to be mass-produced in standard sizes ready for sale. Although the fashion industry developed first in Europe and America, presently it is an international and highly globalized industry, with clothing often designed in one country, manufactured in another, and sold worldwide. For example, an American fashion company might source fabric in China and have the clothes manufactured in Vietnam, finished in Italy, and shipped to a warehouse in the United States for distribution to retail outlets internationally. The fashion industry has long been one of the largest employers. However, due to increase in labor costs it has moved from developed countries to developing particularly China and African countries. Fashion industry employs people across occupation from skilled labour to fashion designers, computer programmers, lawyers, accountants, copywriters, social media directors, and project managers. Manufacturing is only a fraction of the modern fashion industry as it is a highly sophisticated industry involving fashion and market research, brand licensing/intellectual property rights, design, materials engineering, product manufacturing, marketing and finally, distribution

Components of fashion industry

The fashion industry consists of four components/levels:

a) The production of raw materials, principally fibers, textiles, leather and fur.

b) The production of fashion goods by designers, manufacturers, contractors, and others.

c) Marketing in the form of advertising and promotion.

d) Wholesale/Retail sales and e- commerce.

These levels consist of many separate but interdependent sectors. These sectors are Textile Design and Production, Fashion Design and Manufacturing, Fashion Retailing, Marketing and Merchandising, Fashion Shows, and Media and Marketing. Each sector is devoted to the goal of satisfying consumer demand that enable designers, manufacturers, retailers and marketing firms to operate for a profit

STATEMENT OF THE PROBLEM

The fashion market in Nigeria is growing speedily; so also is the growth of competition among designers. As observed by Alabi (2015), Nigeria is a creative hub of talented designers. In all the states of the federation, local fashion stylists are seen with newer and attractive styles on periodic basis. The local designers have the skill to reproduce at better and reduced prices, expensive designs of internationally known design makers. This stiffens the competition in the industry. Today, senators, bankers, celebrities, students, civil servants, etc can be proud to wear clothing and foot wears made by Nigerians for certain occasions. Although the footwear section still has a long way to go in terms of quality, Nigerian designers are making waves in the country and beyond. However, it is disappointing to note that most of these fashion designers lack relevant knowledge of the exact forces behind the behaviour of their consumers and the magnitude of impact the forces exact on fashion consumption. They pay little or no attention to factors that drive positive consumer behaviour towards their products and they think less about customer loyalty, customer word-of-mouth promotion, internationalization as well as technological enhancement. These make it difficult for the designers to gain sustainable competitive advantage and enhanced customer satisfaction locally and internationally. Again, fashion stylists spend little or no resources on marketing researches to find out the trend of global fashion while the few that do, find it difficult to relate global trend to the peculiar environment of Nigerian fashion consumers. Above all, there is an obvious paucity of literature and empirical studies on fashion consumer behaviour in the Nigerian context. This makes it hard for the educated fashion stylists and designers to follow any tailored fashion consumer behaviour model in their production and marketing strategies. It was this wide gap that this present study sought to close. However, the researchers paid attention to clothing and footwear fashion with the Preez (2003) model of apparel shopping behaviour as a guide. This model majored on demographic, socio-cultural and psychological factors. Our study added other factors to suite the peculiarity of the study environment, while concentrating on the psychological factors only.

Business models of fashion industry

The fashion industry is a dynamic in the sense that fashion trends and styles change continuously. Each fashion company responds differently to the changes in fashion trends, distribution and selling of clothes to its customers. The majority of companies choose to follow the latest fashion trends while new entrants try to emphasize quality over quantity by striving for a more sustainable and long- lasting approach. These differences are generally illustrated by two business models, which have emerged over the past few years within the fashion industry, namely the fast fashion and slow fashion model. According to Fletcher fast fashion is time based whereas slow fashion is rather quality-based

FACTORS INFLUENCING FASHION

The main factors which influence fashion can be divided mainly into five different segments:

- Social Factors.
- Cultural Factors.
- Political Factors.
- Environmental Factors.
- Psychological Factors.

FACTORS INFLUENCING FASHION

- SOCIAL FACTOR

Social influence is particularly apparent in the area of clothing and adornment. In. these merchandise categories, most products are nearly equivalent from a func- tional. point of view, and consumers are, in large part, making social identity state- ments with what they buy. Fashion is more than a social process involving clothing and address, but is an expressive appreciation of novelty and individuality, which highlights both economic production and personal consumption. ... Perrine acknowledged the social constructs are being part of not only cultural phenomena, but tradition as well. These factors include-population growth, age distribution, health consciousness, career attitudes and so on. These factors are of particular interest as they have a direct effect on how fashion industry understands customers. The fashion industry is one of those industries that may be most affected by the impact of socio-cultural trends For instance, it has been witnessed for decades that the world population is aging. Such a demographic change may result in a threat for solely teenage oriented apparel firms because the competition for their shrinking segment becomes more intense. However, an opportunity can open up for new or more flexible incumbent fashion retailers. They may focus on more mature customers and offer appropriate sizes and simpler designs with quality durable materials. Another social trend is that customers are more and more concerned about their health, which can be confirmed by a steady increase in individual health expenditur. This may lead to a greater customer interest in the materials used, their origin and their processing methods, demanding more transparency and accountability on behalf of the fashion firms. In this respect, more and more customers have gone 'green' and support sustainable and ethical activities of companies. Besides this, fashion tastes and trends of teenagers and young adults are very diverse and volatile nowadays and are influenced by celebrities and the media. The 'hipster' trend is a recent example and companies may have to decide if they follow such temporary fads or if their business is stable enough to sustain within their usual channels. The media, however, does not only spread trends to customers but also makes aware of scandals and negative publicity about bad Corporate Social Responsibility (CSR) practices like child labor, sweat shops or inhumane working conditions. One example was the incident at the Rana Plaza in Bangladesh in 2013, a factory which makes garments for chains like Primark, where more than 1,100 workers died when the dilapidated building collapsed above their heads. As a result, changes in customer behaviour and attitudes towards fashion companies are increasing the demand to more reporting activities and auditing processes on labour conditions and wages to ensure a fairer treatment of workers.

Political and legal Factors:

These are all about how and to what degree a government intervenes in the economy. This can include - government policy, political stability or instability, foreign trade policy, tax policy, labor law, environmental law, trade restrictions and so on. It is clear from the list above that political factors often have an impact on ease of doing business. Organizations need to be able to respond to the current and anticipated future legislation and adjust their marketing policy accordingly. Legal factors include - health and safety, equal opportunities, advertising standards, consumer rights and laws, product labeling and product safety. It is clear that companies need to know what is and what is not legal in order to trade successfully. If an organization trades globally this becomes a very tricky area to get right as each country has its own set of rules and regulations

ENVIRONMENTAL FACTORS

These factors have come to the forefront by the turn of the century. They have become important due to the increasing scarcity of raw materials, pollution, health hazards, carbon footprint targets set by governments to mitigate climate change, doing business in an ethical and socially responsible way etc. These are just some of the issues marketers are facing within this factor. More and more consumers are demanding that the products they buy are sourced ethically and if possible from a sustainable source. In the environmental dimension of the PESTEL framework several trends can be observed which are likely to have an impact on fashion industry. First of all, climate change and global warming might pose serious challenges to fashion companies in the future, especially within developing countries Events like droughts, tsunamis or floods are often unforeseeable and can harm the growth of cotton and the maintenance of manufacturing facilities. Since many retailers have shifted the production to so- called developing countries in Asia

Fashion industry need to be particularly aware of such environmental risks and create awareness in production units and among workers for such events. Besides, in order to counteract and reduce the consequences of the changing climate, stakeholders are putting pressure on fashion companies to reduce their carbon footprint and incorporate environmental friendly practices alongside their whole supply chain. A related critical debate that has been pursued recently and may continue to be the issue in the future is about the environmental pollution that is attributed to the supply chain activities of companies in the apparel industry. Fashion leaves a great environmental footprint along its supply chain and life cycle. For instance, growing non-organic cotton requires a big amount of chemicals, water and pesticides, which harm human health and have a significant, long-lasting impact on the environment. Besides, overconsumption in the fast-fashion world leads to greater amounts of waste creating disposability problems.

Textile production facilities use a lot of energy, water and chemicals generating contaminated water and toxic volatile emissions. No one wants to eat a meal laced with plastic, but if something doesn't change in our current textile economy, that could soon be a reality. Plastic microfibers, which are like tiny pieces of plastic lint that come off synthetic clothing in the washing machine, are now entering the oceans at a rate of about half a million tons every year - that's equivalent to more than 50 billion plastic bottles. Once in the water, these microfibers are ingested by aquatic wildlife and travel up the food chain where they end up being consumed by humans. This problem is just one of many, highlighted in a report from the Ellen MacArthur Foundation. Entitled "A New Textiles Economy: Redesigning Fashion's Future." The report has garnered support from brands like Stella McCartney, Nike and H&M in addition to the United Nations and organizations like the Sustainable Apparel Coalition and the C&A Foundation .

The House of Commons environmental audit committee in U K has launched an inquiry to explore the carbon impact, resource use and water footprint of clothing throughout its lifecycle and supply chain. The committee has observed that the globalised market for fashion manufacturing has facilitated a "fast fashion" phenomenon; a proliferation of cheap and cheerful clothing, with quick turnover that encourages consumers to keep buying. The key to the inquiry is how consumers could be encouraged to buy fewer clothes, reuse clothes and think about how best to dispose of clothes when they are no longer wanted. An estimated 300,000 tonnes of fashion waste goes straight into landfill each year in U K, despite growing efforts to encourage consumers to recycle their worn and unwanted clothing. It is for these reasons more and more consumers, governments and other stakeholders demand more sustainable and ethical practices in daily business operations. If fashion companies want to maintain loyal customers, they need to reduce their impact on the environment and invest in sustainable and eco-friendly practices in order to reduce waste and minimize the pollution of water and air

PSYCHOLOGICAL FACTOR

Many psychological factors help explain what motivates us to be fashionable. These include conformity, desires for variety seeking, the need to express personal creativity, and sexual attraction. For example, many consumers seem to have a need for uniqueness. They want to be different (though not necessarily too different!). As a result, people may conform to the basic outlines of a fashion, but still improvise to make a personal statement within these general guidelines.

One of the earliest theories of fashion psychology argued that "shifting erogenous zones" (sexually arousing areas of the body) accounted for fashion changes, and that different zones become the object of interest because they reflect societal trends. For example, it was common for Renaissance-era women to drape their abdomens in fabrics to give a swollen appearance; successful childbearing was a priority in the disease-ridden 14th and 15th centuries. Numerous studies have looked at how variations in clothing influence observers' responses. For example, one study found that men tended to leave higher tips for waitresses who wore red tops. The "dress for success" phenomenon illustrates the widespread belief that appearance directly impacts the way people are treated.

Accelerating factors of fashion

Good economic conditions: Accelerate fashion movement. ... At the introduction stage of the fashion cycle, new styles are: Usually accepted by only a small number of fashion leaders

Factors that Speed Up Fashion Cycle Movement

- Mass media, modern communications.
- Good economic conditions.
- Increased competition.
- Technological advances.
- Social and physical mobility.
- More leisure time.
- Higher levels of education.
- Changing roles of women.

Decceleration factor in fashion

The deceleration phase: the growth rate gradually decreases along limitation of nutrient availability and accumulation of metabolized products. Factors that influence the effects of deceleration are the initial rate of speed, the distance covered and time consumed in deceleration, the direction of forces, and the area of distribution

FASHION DESIGNER

Fashion designers are responsible for creating looks for individual garments, involving shape, color, fabric, trimming, and more. ... They consider who is likely to wear a garment and the situations in which it will be worn, and they work within a wide range of materials, colors, patterns and styles.

Different types of Fashion Designers that exist!

- Haute Couture Designers.
- Pret-a-porter Designers.
- Mass Market Designers.
- Sportwear Designers.
- Evening Wear Designers.
- Fashion accessory Designers.
- Footwear Designers.
- Kidswear Designers.

CLASSICIST FASHION DESIGNER

A classic fashion is a style that lasts for several seasons, sometimes even years, and is accepted by a wide range of people. Classics are those styles that you don’t even have to think about. You just know they will be acceptable from one year to the next. Running shoes are a good example of a classic style.

FASHION INFLUENCER

A fashion influencer is a personality that has a large number of followers on social media, creates mainly fashion content and has the power to influence the opinion and purchase behavior of others with their recommendations.

FASHION STUDIO

A fashion design studio is a workplace for designers to conceptualize, design, and possibly create apparel and relevant products. ... In the fashion studios, fashion designers, artisans and illustrators engage in conceiving, designing and developing new clothing, shoes, jewelry, or fashion accessories.

STUDIO LINE FASHION

A clothing line refers to "all of the clothing" a fashion company produces for a specific category. A clothing collection generally refers to clothing produced for a particular season. For example, "the designers clothing line is outstanding". This can refer to the entire product range for a long length of time.

CONCLUSION

Though fast fashion model is well established, however, due to environmental issues and social values related to business ethics, the slow fashion model is gaining an edge over. Business environment is an alternative term to business marketing. Among the three factors, macro factors known as PESTEL are purely of external nature need to be carefully understood and researched by the fashion industry for carrying out the business in ethical and environmentally friendly way for its sustainability. Technology is playing a great role in the marketing of fashion products but is also posing a threat of competition. Therefore, creating a brand image based on ethics and providing environmentally friendly products has become essential for the survival in the global fashion industry.

CHAPTER II

LEGENDARY FASHION DESIGNERS

INTRODUCTION

Fashion design is the art of applying design, aesthetics, clothing construction and natural beauty to clothing and its accessories. It is influenced by culture and different trends, and has varied over time and place.

It's the job of the fashion designer to design garments, choose fabrics and patterns, and guide manufacturers on how to make original fashion pieces. As a fashion designer, your other duties might include: Keeping up-to-date with current fashion trends to keep their fashion brand relevant.

Fashion design can generally be divided into tiers, and while there exists some overlap and subcategorization, there are five main types of fashion design. The five types of fashion design are: Haute Couture Fashion. Luxury Fashion.

Fashion industry has been undergone substantial transformation over the years. Fashion houses are no longer working with two collections per year – Fall/Winter and Spring/Summer. Many fashion professionals are working with multiple collections and deliveries every season. They are constantly searching for fresh idea and creating new products in order to meet their customer's aspirations. 'Fast fashion' companies have been successfully using various strategies to reduce the production lead time, increase their competitive advantage and expedite the design process. This research project was undertaken to examine the relationship between designer (ideation), product (innovative design) and consumer (aspirations). Consumption culture was discussed and design issues were identified in this paper. Based on cross-disciplinary literature, a conceptual design model was developed. This paper is attempted to identify research opportunities for the future, offer recommendations for fashion practitioners.

INTERNATIONALFASHIONDESIGNER

Top 10 fashion Designers of the world

- Coco Chanel (1883-1971)
- Calvin Klein (Born 1942)
- Donatella Versace (Born 1955)
- Giorgio Armani (Born 1934)
- Ralph Lauren (Born 1939)
- Marc Jacobs (Born 1963)
- Donna Karan (Born 1948)
- Christian Dior (1905-1957)

INTERNATIONAL DESIGNER

Designers who are popular in the international fashion market are called as International Fashion designers with high grades and quality

- **YVES SAINT LAURENT**

A French fashion designer who, in 1962, founded his eponymous fashion label. He is regarded as being among the foremost fashion designers of the twentieth century. In 1985, Caroline Milbank wrote, The most consistently celebrated and influential designer of the past twenty-five years, Yves Saint Laurent can be credited with both spurring the couture's rise from its 1960s ashes and with finally rendering ready-to-wear reputable. He developed his style to accommodate the changes in fashion during that period. He approached his aesthetic from a different perspective by helping women find confidence by looking both comfortable and elegant at the same time. He is also credited with having introduced the "Le Smoking" tuxedo suit for women and was known for his use of non-European cultural references and of diverse models.

HISTORY

Saint Laurent was born on 1 August 1936, in Oran, French Algeria, to French parents, Charles and Lucienne Andrée Mathieu-Saint-Laurent. He grew up in a villa by the Mediterranean with his two younger sisters, Michèle and Brigitte. Saint Laurent liked to create intricate paper dolls, and by his early teen years, he was designing dresses for his mother and sisters. At the age of 17, Saint Laurent moved to Paris and enrolled at the Chambre Syndicale de la Haute Couture, where his designs quickly gained notice. Michel De Brunhoff, the editor of French Vogue, introduced Saint Laurent to designer Christian Dior, a giant in the fashion world. "Dior fascinated me," Saint Laurent later recalled. "I couldn't speak in front of him. He taught me the basis of my art. Whatever was to happen next, I never forgot the years I spent at his side." Under Dior's tutelage, Saint Laurent's style continued to mature and gain even more notice.

CARRIER

In 1953, Saint Laurent submitted three sketches to a contest for young fashion designers organized by the International Wool Secretariat. Saint Laurent won first place. Subsequently, he was invited to attend the awards ceremony held in Paris in December of that same year. During his stay in Paris, Saint Laurent met Michel de Brunhoff (who was then editor-in-chief of the French edition of Vogue magazine and a connection to his father). De Brunhoff, known by some as a considerate person who encouraged new talent, was impressed by the sketches that Saint Laurent brought with him and suggested he should intend to become a fashion designer. Saint Laurent would eventually consider a course of study at the Chambre Syndicale de la Haute Couture, the council which regulates the haute couture industry and provides training to its employees. Saint Laurent followed his advice and, leaving Oran for Paris after graduation, began his studies there and eventually graduated as a star pupil. Later, that same year, he entered the International Wool Secretariat competition again and won, beating out his friend Fernando Sánchez and young German student Karl Lagerfeld. Shortly after his win, he brought a number of sketches to de Brunhoff who recognized close similarities to sketches he had been shown that morning by Christian Dior. Knowing that Dior had created the sketches that morning and that the young man could not have seen them, de Brunhoff sent him to Dior, who hired him on the spot.

Although Dior recognised his talent immediately, Saint Laurent spent his first year at the House of Dior on mundane tasks, such as decorating the studio and designing accessories. Eventually, however, he was allowed to submit sketches for the couture collection; with every passing season, more of his sketches were accepted by Dior. In August 1957, Dior met with Saint Laurent's mother to tell her that he had chosen Saint Laurent to succeed him as a designer. His mother later said that she had been confused by the remark, as Dior was only 52 years old at the time. Both she and her son were surprised when in October of that year Dior died at a health spa in northern Italy of a massive heart attack.

In 1957, Saint Laurent found himself at age 21 the head designer of the House of Dior. His spring 1958 collection almost certainly saved the enterprise from financial ruin. The simple, flaring lines of his first collection for Dior,[14] called the Trapeze line, a variation of Dior's 1955 A-Line, catapulted him to international stardom. Dresses in the collection featured a narrow shoulder that flared gently to a hem that just covered the knee. At that time, he shortened his surname to Saint Laurent because the international press found his hyphenated triple name difficult to express.

His fall 1958 collection was not greeted with the same level of approval as his first collection and later collections for the House of Dior featuring hobble skirts and beatnik fashions were savaged by the press.

In 1959, he was chosen by Farah Diba, who was a student in Paris, to design her wedding dress for her marriage to the Shah of Iran.

In 1960, Saint Laurent found himself conscripted to serve in the French Army during the Algerian War of Independence. Alice Rawsthorn writes that there was speculation at the time that Marcel Boussac, the owner of the House of Dior and a powerful press baron, had put pressure on the government not to conscript Saint Laurent in 1958 and 1959, but after the disastrous 1958 season, reversed course and asked that the designer be conscripted so that he could be replaced.

- **VALENTINO**

Valentino S.p.A. is an Italian luxury fashion house founded in 1960 by Valentino Garavani and part of Valentino Fashion Group.

Valentino, in full **Valentino Clemente Ludovico Garavani,** (born May 11, 1932, Voghera, Italy), Italian fashion designer known for garments in his trademark "Valentino red" (*rosso Valentino*) and whose style was described as jet-set chic.

As a child, Valentino was interested in both fashion and art. In 1949 he left his home in Voghera, a small town between Turin and Milan, to study fashion sketching at Milan's Santa Maria Institute. He also enrolled in a Berlitz French course, which proved useful when in 1949 he moved to Paris to attend the École des Beaux-Arts and to study fashion at a school run by the Chambre Syndicale, the French fashion governing body. At that time the Paris fashion scene was a hostile environment for foreigners, particularly Italians. But Valentino won a competition for fashion design run by the International Wool Secretariat (the same prize that Yves Saint Laurent and Karl Lagerfeld won in subsequent years), and his prize led to a job at the French couture house of Jean Dessès.

HISTORY

In 1957 Guy Laroche, an illustrator at Dessès, decided to set up his own fashion house, and Valentino worked with him for two years. In 1959 Valentino returned to Rome and, with the financial backing of his father, presented his first collection in his own salon on Via Condotti. Elizabeth Taylor, who was in Rome shooting *Cleopatra* at the time, spotted Valentino's work and placed her order for a white dress, which she wore for the world premiere of *Spartacus*. Valentino's fate was sealed. In 1960 Valentino met Giancarlo Giametti, an architecture student, who became his partner in charge of the commercial side of the business. Valentino debuted his first couture fashion line in 1962 at the Pitti Palace in Florence and began to establish an international reputation. Well-known personalities soon sought him out for designs, including Belgian Queen Paola, Princess Margaret of England, Audrey Hepburn, and Jacqueline Kennedy. Valentino designed many dresses for Kennedy, including the dress she wore to her husband's funeral in 1963 and then, in 1968, a dress for her wedding to Aristotle Onassis.

Though Valentino's trademark colour was red, it was a 1967 collection entirely of white, ivory, and beige clothes—his "no colour" collection—that thrust him into the fashion spotlight and for which he was awarded the Neiman Marcus Award. That collection stood in stark contrast to the bold psychedelic patterns of the time. With the "no colour" collection he also launched his trademark V logo. In 1969 he opened his first ready-to-wear shop in Milan. He opened stores in New York City and Rome the following year. The designer went on to enjoy an extremely successful and illustrious career, serving high society and the entertainment world. He and Giametti sold the company in 1998, though Valentino remained the designer. In 2006 he received the French Legion of Honour medal, and he retired in 2008. That year he was the subject of the documentary*Valentino: The Last Emperor.*

- **PIERRE CARDIN**

Pietro Costante Cardin(2 July 1922 – 29 December 2020),was an Italian-born naturalised-Frenchfashion designer. He is known for what were his avant-garde style and Space Age designs. He preferred geometric shapes and motifs, often ignoring the female form. He advanced into unisex fashions, sometimes experimental, and not always practical. He founded his fashion house in 1950 and introduced the "bubble dress" in 1954.

He was designated a UNESCO Goodwill Ambassador in 1991and a United Nations FAO Goodwill Ambassador in 2009.

HISTORY

Cardin was born near Treviso in northern Italy, the son of Maria Montagner and Alessandro Cardin.His parents were wealthy wine merchants, but lost their fortune in World War I.To escape the blackshirts they left Italy and settled in Saint-Étienne, France in 1924 along with his ten siblings. His father wanted him to study architecture, but from childhood he was interested in dressmaking.

Cardin moved to Paris in 1945. There, he studied architecture and worked with the fashion house of Paquin after World War II. He worked with Elsa Schiaparelli until he became head of Christian Dior's tailleure atelier in 1947, but was denied work at Balenciaga.

Cardin founded his own fashion house in 1950.His career was launched when he designed about 30 of the costumes for a masquerade ball in Venice, hosted by Carlos de Beistegui in 1951. Cardin inaugurated his haute couture output in 1953 with his first collection of women's clothing and became a member of the Chambre Syndicale, a French association of haute couture designers.The following year he opened his first boutique Eve and introduced the "bubble dress", which is a short-skirted, bubble-shaped dress made by bias-cutting over a stiffened base. He was the first couturier to turn to Japan as a high fashion market when he travelled there in 1957.

As haute couture began to decline, ready-to-wear ('prêt-à-porter') soared as well as Cardin's designs. He was the first to combine the "mini" and the "maxi" skirts of the 1970s by introducing a new hemline that had long pom-pom panels or fringes.

Beginning in the 1970s, Cardin set another new trend: "mod chic". This trend holds true for the form or for a combination of forms, which did not exist at the time. He was the first to combine extremely short and ankle-length pieces. He made dresses with slits and batwing sleeves with novel dimensions and mixed circular movement and gypsy skirts with structured tops. These creations allowed for the geometric shapes that captivated him to be contrasted, with both circular and straight lines. Cardin became an icon for starting this popular fashion movement of the early 1970s.

Inspired by space travel and exploration, Cardin visited NASA (the National Aeronautics and Space Administration) in 1970, where he tried on the original spacesuit worn by the first human to set foot on the moon, Neil Armstrong.Cardin designed spacesuits for NASA in 1970.

Cardin resigned from the Chambre Syndicale in 1966 and began showing his collections in his own venue.He also designed uniforms for Pakistan International Airlines, which were introduced from 1966 to 1971 and became an instant hit.

In 1971, Cardin redesigned the Barong Tagalog, a national costume of the Philippines, by opening the front, removing the cuffs that needed cufflinks, flaring the sleeves, and minimizing the embroidery. It was also tapered to the body, in contrast with the traditional loose-fitting design, and it also had a thicker collar with sharp and pointed cuffs. A straight-cut design was favored by PresidentFerdinand Marcos.

In 1975, Cardin opened his first furniture boutique on the Rue du Faubourg Saint-Honoré.In 1977, 1979, and 1983, he was awarded the Cartier Golden Thimble by French haute couture for the most creative collection of the season.He was a member of the Chambre Syndicale de la Haute Couture et du Prêt-à-Porter from 1953 to 1993.

Like many other designers today, Cardin decided in 1994 to show his collection only to a small circle of selected clients and journalists. After a break of 15 years, he showed a new collection to a group of 150 journalists at his bubble home in Cannes.

A biography titled Pierre Cardin, his fabulous destiny was written by Sylvana Lorenz.

ABOUT THE BRAND

Pierre Cardin used his name as a brand, initially a prestigious fashion brand, then in the 1960s extended successfully into perfumes and cosmetics. From about 1988 the brand was licensed extensively, and appeared on "wildly nonadjacent products such as baseball caps and cigarettes".

A 2005 article in the Harvard Business Review commented that the extension into perfumes and cosmetics was successful as the premium nature of the Pierre Cardin brand transferred well into these new, adjacent categories, but that the owners of the brand mistakenly attributed this to the brand's strength rather than to its fit with the new product categories.The extensive licensing eroded the brand's credibility, but brought in much revenue; in 1986 Women's Wear Daily (WWD) estimated Cardin's annual income at over US$10 million.

In 1995, quotes from WWD included "Pierre Cardin—he has sold his name for toilet paper. At what point do you lose your identity?" and "Cardin's cachet crashed when his name appeared on everything from key chains to pencil holders". However, the Cardin name was still very profitable, although the indiscriminate licensing approach was considered a failure.

In 2011, Cardin tried to sell his business, valuing it at €1 billion, although the Wall Street Journal considered it to be worth about a fifth of that amount. Ultimately he did not sell the brand

- **RALPH LAUREN**

An American fashion designer, philanthropist, and billionaire businessman, best known for the Ralph Lauren Corporation, a global multibillion-dollar enterprise. He has become well known for his collection of rare automobiles, some of which have been displayed in museum exhibits. Lauren stepped down as CEO of the company in September 2015 but remains executive chairman and chief creative officer. As of 2019, Forbes estimates his wealth at $6.3 billion, which makes Ralph Lauren the 102nd richest person in America.

Drawing on his interests in sports, Lauren named his first full line of menswear 'Polo' in 1968. He worked out of a single "drawer" from a showroom in the Empire State Building and made deliveries to stores himself. By 1969, the Manhattan department store Bloomingdale's sold Lauren's men's line exclusively. It was the first time that Bloomingdale's had given a designer their own in-store boutique.

In 1971, Ralph Lauren Corporation launched a line of tailored shirts for women, which introduced the Polo player emblem to the world for the first time, appearing on the shirt's cuff. The first full women's collection was launched the following year. In 1971 Lauren also opened a store on Rodeo Drive in Beverly Hills, California; this was the first freestanding store for an American designer.

In 1972, the Ralph Lauren Corporation introduced a signature cotton mesh Polo shirt in various colors. Featuring the polo player logo at the chest, the shirt became emblematic of the preppy look—one of Ralph Lauren's signature styles. The tagline for the ad campaign was: "Every team has its color – Polo has seventeen."

In 1974, he outfitted the male cast of The Great Gatsby in costumes from his Polo line – a 1920s-style series of men's suits and sweaters, except for the pink suit which Lauren designed especially for Robert Redford's Jay Gatsby. In 1977, Diane Keaton and Woody Allen wore Lauren's clothes throughout their Oscar-winning film, Annie Hall.

What does Ralph Lauren sell?

Ralph Lauren Corporation is an American publicly traded fashion company that was founded in 1967 by American fashion designer Ralph Lauren.

Formerly

Polo Ralph Lauren Corporation

Products

Luxury clothing Footwear Fragrances Housewares Furniture Jewelry

Services

Tailoring

Revenue

US$6.182 billion (2018)

- **KARL LAGERFIELD**

He was known as the creative director of the French fashion house Chanel, a position held from 1983 until his death, and was also creative director of the Italian fur and leather goods fashion house Fendi, and of his own eponymous fashion label. He collaborated on a variety of fashion and art-related projects.

Lagerfeld was recognized for his signature white hair, black sunglasses, fingerless gloves, and high, starched, detachable collars.

HISTORY

Lagerfeld was born on 10 September 1933 in Hamburg, to Elisabeth (née Bahlmann) and businessman Otto Lagerfeld.His father owned a company that produced and imported evaporated milk; while his maternal grandfather, Karl Bahlmann, was a local politician for the Catholic Centre Party. His family belonged to the Old Catholic Church. When Lagerfeld's mother met his father, she was a lingerie saleswoman from Berlin. His parents married in 1930.

Lagerfeld was known to misrepresent his birth year, claiming to be younger than his actual age, and to misrepresent his parents' background. For example, he claimed that he was born in 1938 to "Elisabeth of Germany" and Otto Ludwig Lagerfeldt . These claims have been conclusively proven to be false, as his father was from Hamburg and spent his entire life in Germany, with no Swedish connection. There is also no evidence that his mother Elisabeth Bahlmann, the daughter of a middle-class local politician, called herself "Elisabeth of Germany". He was known to insist that no one knows his real birth date. In an interview on French television in February 2009, Lagerfeld said that he was "born neither in 1933 nor 1938".

In April 2013, he finally declared that he was born in 1935. A birth announcement was, however, published by his parents in 1933, and the baptismal register in Hamburg also lists him as born in that year, showing that he was born on 10 September 1933. Bild am Sonntag published his baptismal records in 2008 and interviewed his teacher and a classmate, who both confirmed that he was born in 1933. The same was later confirmed by his death record. Despite that, Karl Lagerfeld announced publicly that he was celebrating his "70th birthday" on 10 September 2008, despite actually turning 75.

His older sister, Martha Christiane "Christel", was born in 1931. Lagerfeld had an older half-sister, Theodora Dorothea "Thea", from his father's first marriage. His family name has been spelled both Lagerfeldt (with a "t") and Lagerfeld. Like his father, he used the spelling Lagerfeld, considering it to "sound more commercial".

His family was mainly shielded from the deprivations of World War II due to his father's business interests in Germany through the firm Glücksklee-Milch GmbH. His father had been in San Francisco during the 1906 earthquake.

As a child, he showed great interest in visual arts, and former schoolmates recalled that he was always making sketches "no matter what we were doing in class".Lagerfeld told interviewers that he learned much more by constantly visiting the Kunsthalle Hamburg museum than he ever did in school.

FASHION CARRIER

In 2002, Lagerfeld asked Renzo Rosso, the founder of Diesel, to collaborate with him on a special denim collection for the Lagerfeld Gallery. The collection, Lagerfeld Gallery by Diesel, was co-designed by Lagerfeld and then developed by Diesel's creative team, under the supervision of Rosso. It consisted of five pieces that were presented during the designer's catwalk shows during Paris Fashion Weekand then sold in highly limited editions at the Lagerfeld Galleries in Paris and Monaco and at the Diesel Denim Galleries in New York and Tokyo. During the first week of sales in New York, more than 90% of the trousers were sold out, even though prices ranged from $240 to $1,840. In a statement after the show in Paris, Rosso said: "I am honored to have met this fashion icon of our time. Karl represents creativity, tradition and challenge, and the fact that he thought of Diesel for this collaboration is a great gift and acknowledgement of our reputation as the prêt-à-porter of casual wear".

In December 2006, Lagerfeld announced the launch of a new collection for men and women dubbed K Karl Lagerfeld, which included fitted T-shirts and a wide range of jeans.In September 2010, the Couture Council of The Museum at the Fashion Institute of Technology presented Lagerfeld with an award created for him, The Couture Council Fashion Visionary Award, at a benefit luncheon at Avery Fisher Hall, in New York City. In November 2010, Lagerfeld and Swedish crystal manufacturer Orrefors announced a collaboration to design a crystal art collection. The first collection was launched in spring 2011, called Orrefors by Karl Lagerfeld.

In 2014, Palm Beach Modern Auctions announced that many of Lagerfeld's early sketches for the House of Tiziani in Rome would be sold.

Lagerfeld's work in fashion houses garnered him to be considered the Chameleon of fashion. Said by Anna Sui and Clare Waight Keller, they emphasized Lagerfeld's ability to elevate the rich history of fashion houses into the modern-day context.

COLLECTION

The final Chanel collection completed before his death had an Alpine theme of après-ski clothing. As Lagerfeld requested not to have any type of funeral, the show only included a moment of silence in his honor and chairs emblazoned with his image next to Coco Chanel with the saying "the beat goes on". Although Lagerfeld shunned any emotional reactions around the idea of his death, some models could be seen crying on the runway, as well as audience members.

Brands under him:

- Cloe
- H&M
- Fendi etc

- **DONNA KAREN**

Donna Karan also known as "DK", is an American fashion designer and the creator of the Donna Karan New York and DKNY clothing labels

HISTORY

Karan began her career as an assistant designer with Anne Klein in the late 1960s, where she was promoted to associate designer in 1971. As Klein's assistant, Karan was a participant in The Battle of Versailles Fashion Show on November 28, 1973. When Klein herself died in 1974, Takihyo Corporation of Japan became the new owner and Karan, together with her former classmate and friend Louis Dell'Olio, became head designer of the house. In 1984, Karan left Anne Klein and, together with her then husband Stephan Weiss and Takihyo Corporation, started her own business "to design modern clothes for modern people". She showed her first women's clothing collection in 1985.

Karan became well known for her 'Essentials' line, initially offering seven easy pieces centered around the bodysuit which could all be mixed and matched, and created a fully integrated wardrobe with her First Collection in 1985. Karan always insisted that she would design only clothes like jersey dresses and opaque Lycra tights that she would wear herself.

In 1988, Karan, nicknamed The Queen Of Seventh Avenue,extended her women's 'Donna Karan New York' line by creating a less expensive clothing line for younger women, called DKNY. Two years later, she created DKNY Jeans, a denim-inspired collection. DKNY for men was launched in 1992, one year after the 'Signature' line for men had been presented. In 1992, Karan also released her "cold shoulder" dress, a jersey long-sleeved dress which featured deep cutouts at the shoulders to reveal the skin beneath.

Karan left her CEO position in 1997, but continued as chairwoman and designer for the Donna Karan line. After 2002, Karan's designer contributions became less and less. In August 2008, Karan relaunched her discontinued fragrance lines from the 1990s.

AWARDS

- 1977: Coty American Fashion Critics' Award
- 1982: Coty American Fashion Critics' Award (together with Louis Dell'Ollio for Anne Klein)
- 1984: Inducted into the Coty Hall Of Fame.
- 1985, 1986, 1987: special CFDA awards
- 1992: Menswear Designer of the Year by the Council of Fashion Designers of America (CFDA)
- 1990, 1996: Womenswear Designer of the Year by the CFDA
- 2004: Lifetime Achievement Award by the CFDA
- 1994:Golden Plate Award of the American Academy of Achievement

DKNY Spring 2012

In 2015, Donna Karan announced that she would be stepping down as head of her eponymous company to focus on her lifestyle brand, Urban Zen, established by Karan in 2007.

- **GEORGIO ARMANI**

An Italian fashion designer. He first gained notoriety working for Cerruti and then for many others, including Allegri, Bagutta and Hilton. He formed his company, Armani, in 1975, which eventually diversified into music, sport and luxury hotels. By 2001 Armani was acclaimed as the most successful designer of Italian origin, and is credited with pioneering red-carpet fashion. In 2010, he opened the Armani Hotel in Burj Khalifa, the world's tallest building. He is also the richest openly LGBT person in the world. According to Bloomberg Billionaires Index, Armani has an estimated net worth of US$9.53 billion, as of 2021.

CARRIER

After his stint in the armed forces, Armani found a job as a window dresser at La Rinascente, a department store in Milan in 1957. He went on to become a seller for the menswear department, in which capacity he gained valuable experience in the marketing aspect of the fashion industry.In the mid-1960s, Armani moved to the Nino Cerruti company, where he designed menswear. His skills were in demand, and for the next decade, while continuing to work for Cerutti, Armani also freelanced, contributing designs to as many as ten manufacturers at a time. In the late 1960s, Armani met Sergio Galeotti, an architectural draftsman, which marked the beginning of a personal and professional relationship that lasted for many years. In 1973, Galeotti persuaded him to open a design office in Milan, at 37 Corso Venezia. This led to a period of extensive collaboration, during which Armani worked as a freelance designer for a number of fashion houses, including Allegri, Bagutta, Hilton, Sicons, Gibò, Montedoro, and Tendresse. The international press was quick to acknowledge Armani's importance following the runway shows at the Sala Bianca in the Pitti Palace in Florence. The experience provided Armani with an opportunity to develop his own style in new ways. He was now ready to devote his energy to his own label, and on July 24, 1975, he founded Giorgio Armani S.p.A. in Milan, with his friend Galeotti. In October of that same year, he presented his first collection of men's ready-to-wear for Spring and Summer 1976 under his own name. He also produced a women's line for the same season.

Armani established an innovative relationship with the fashion industry, characterized by the 1978 agreement with Gruppo Finanzario Tessile (GFT), which made it possible to produce luxury ready-to-wear in a manufacturing environment under the attentive supervision of the company's designer. In 1979, after founding the Giorgio Armani Corporation, Armani began producing for the United States and introduced the Main line for men and women. The label became one of the leading names in international fashion with the introduction of several new product lines, including G. A. Le Collezioni, Giorgio Armani Underwear and Swimwear, and Giorgio Armani Accessories. In the early 1980s the company signed an important agreement with L'Oréal to create perfumes and introduced the Armani Junior, Armani Jeans, and Emporio Armani lines, followed in 1982 by the introduction of Emporio Underwear, Swimwear, and Accessories. A new store was opened in Milan for the Emporio line, followed by the first Giorgio Armani boutique. Armani's concern for the end user culminated in the development of a more youthful product with the same level of stylistic quality as his high-end line, but at a more accessible price.

Because of the democratic nature of the Emporio line, Armani felt that he had to make use of new and unconventional advertising methods. These included television spots and enormous street ads, together with a house magazine that was sent out by mail to consumers, faithful Armani Eagle wearers. Armani also felt that a relationship with the cinema was essential, both for promotional reasons and for the stimulus to creativity. He designed the costumes for American Gigolo (1980),the success of which led to a long-term collaboration with the world of film. Armani designed costumes for more than one hundred films, one of the most important of which was The Untouchables (1987).

In 1983 the designer modified his agreement with GFT. They began to produce both the Mani line for the United States and his high-end ready-to-wear line, rechristened Borgonuovo 21, after the address of the company's headquarters. During the late 1980s, despite Galeotti's death in 1985, Armani continued to expand commercial horizons and licensing agreements. He opened Armani Japan and introduced a line of eyeglasses (1988), socks (1987), a gift collection (1989), and a new "basic" men's and women's line for America known as A/X Armani Exchange (1991). After the frenetic expansion of the 1990s (sportswear, watches, eyeglasses, cosmetics, home, and new accessories collections), 2000, the twenty-fifth anniversary of the brand, saw a flurry of investment activity, including stock sales and the acquisition of new manufacturing capacity intended to increase Armani's control over the quality and distribution of his products.

Armani's men's and women's skiwear and ski casualwear line was developed in 1995. His 1991 project, A/X: Armani Exchange, represented Armani's attempt to break into the American mass market, offering lower prices for relaxed chic clothes.

In 1996 his long-time friend Eric Clapton composed songs for Armani's fashion shows and has since dressed in Armani. Later that year Clapton opened two Emporio Armani stores in New York City.In 1998 Armani hosted a party for Clapton's Crossroads guitar auction.

Armani also prepared to break into the Chinese market by opening up his first store in that country in 1998. The small shop in Beijing was followed by a flagship store in Shanghai in 2004 and plans for 40 by 2011. In 2000, Giorgio Armani SpA was introducing new lines of cosmetics and home furnishings, and expanding its line of accessories. At the same time, the Guggenheim Museum in New York hosted an exhibition of Armani's work – a first for a living designer – with average attendance of 29,000 a week.

In 2008, Armani designed the bullfighting costume, called the "Goyesco", worn by Spanish bullfighter Cayetano Rivera Ordóñez at the "Corrida Goyesca" in Ronda, Spain. They have also collaborated on several fashion shows and other events.

As of 2009, Armani has a retail network of 60 Giorgio Armani boutiques, 11 Collezioni, 122 Emporio Armani, 94 A/X Armani Exchange, 1 Giorgio Armani Accessori, and 13 Armani Junior stores spread over 37 different countries. He has an annual turnover of $1.6 billion and a personal fortune of $8.1 billion as of 2017.

In 2001 Armani was acclaimed as the most successful designer of Italian origin.

Giorgio Armani S.p.A. (pronounced [ˈdʒordʒo arˈmaːni ˈspa]), commonly known as Armani, is an Italian luxury fashion house founded by Giorgio Armani which designs, manufactures, distributes and retails haute couture, ready-to-wear, leather goods, shoes, watches, jewelry, accessories, eyewear, cosmetics and home

- **COCO CHANEL**

Gabrielle Bonheur Chanel, (born August 19, 1883, Saumur, France—died January 10, 1971, Paris), French fashion designer who ruled Parisian haute couture for almost six decades. Her elegantly casual designs inspired women of fashion to abandon the complicated, uncomfortable clothes—such as petticoats and corsets—that were prevalent in 19th-century dress. Among her now-classic innovations were the Chanel suit, the quilted purse, costume jewelry, and the "little black dress."

HISTORY

Chanel was born into poverty in the French countryside; her mother died, and her father abandoned her to an orphanage. After a brief stint as a shopgirl, Chanel worked for a few years as a café singer. She later became associated with a few wealthy men and in 1913, with financial assistance from one of them, Arthur ("Boy") Capel, opened a tiny millinery shop in Deauville, France, where she also sold simple sportswear, such as jersey sweaters. Within five years her original use of jersey fabric to create a "poor girl" look had attracted the attention of influential wealthy women seeking relief from the prevalent corseted styles. Faithful to her maxim that "luxury must be comfortable, otherwise it is not luxury," Chanel's designs stressed simplicity and comfort and revolutionized the fashion industry. By the late 1920s the Chanel industries were reportedly worth millions and employed more than 2,000 people, not only in her couture house but also in a perfume laboratory, a textile mill, and a jewelry workshop.

The financial basis of this empire was Chanel No. 5, the phenomenally successful perfume she introduced in 1921 with the help of Ernst Beaux, one of the most-talented perfume creators in France. It has been said that the perfume got its name from the series of scents that Beaux created for Chanel to sample—she chose the fifth, a combination of jasmine and several other floral scents that was more complex and mysterious than the single-scented perfumes then on the market. That Chanel was the first major fashion designer to introduce a perfume and that she replaced the typical perfume packaging with a simple and sleek bottle also added to the scent's success. She partnered with businessmen Théophile Bader of the Galeries Lafayette department store and Pierre Wertheimer of the Bourjois cosmetics company, who both agreed to help her produce more of her fragrance and to market it in exchange for a share of the profits. After signing a contract wherein she received only 10 percent of the royalties, Chanel enacted a series of lawsuits in the ensuing decades to regain control of her signature fragrance. Although she was never able to renegotiate the terms of her contract to increase her royalties, Chanel nonetheless made a considerable profit from the perfume.

Chanel closed her couture house in 1939 with the outbreak of World War II. Her associations with a German diplomat during the Nazi occupation tainted her reputation, and she did not return to fashion until 1954. That year she introduced her highly copied suit design: a collarless, braid-trimmed cardigan jacket with a graceful skirt. She also introduced bell-bottomed pants and other innovations while always retaining a clean classic look.

After her death in 1971, Chanel's couture house was led by a series of designers, with Karl Lagerfeld's tenure (1983–2019) being the longest and most influential. Chanel's shrewd understanding of women's fashion needs, her enterprising ambition, and the romantic aspects of her life—her rise from rags to riches and her sensational love affairs—continued to inspire numerous biographical books, films, and plays, including the 1970 Broadway musical *Coco* starring Katharine Hepburn.

PRODUCTS

Its products cover clothes, fragrances, handbags and watches. The brand is most famous for its "little black dress", the Chanel No. 5 perfume and the Chanel Suit.

- **CALVIN KLIEN**

An American fashion designer who launched the company that would later become Calvin Klein Inc., in 1968. In addition to clothing, he also has given his name to a range of perfumes, watches, and jewellery.

HISTORY

Calvin Klein was one of several design leaders raised in the Jewish community in the Bronx, along with Robert Denning and Ralph Lauren. He became a protégé of Baron de Gunzburg through whose introductions he became the toast of the New York elite fashion scene even before he had his first mainstream success with the launch of his first jeans line. He was immediately recognized for his talent after his first major showing at New York Fashion Week.

In 1968, Klein founded Calvin Klein Limited, a coat shop in the York Hotel in New York City, with $10,000. The first Calvin Klein collection was a line of "youthful, understated coats and dresses" featured at the New York City store Bonwit Teller.

In September 1969, Klein appeared on the cover of Vogue magazine

1970s

By 1971, Klein had added sportswear, classic blazers, and lingerie to his women's collection

In 1973, he received his first Coty American Fashion Critics' Award for his 74-piece womenswear collection – the youngest recipient at that time. Klein won the award again in 1974 and 1975 By 1977, annual revenues had increased to $30 million (equivalent to $128 million in 2022), and Klein had licenses for scarves, shoes, belts, furs, sunglasses, and bedsheets. Klein and Schwartz were making $4 million each. After the company signed licenses for cosmetics, jeans, and menswear, Klein's annual retail volume was estimatedat $100 million (equivalent to $427 million in 2022). In 1978, Klein claimed sales of 200,000 pairs of his famous jeans the first week they were on the market. By 1981, Fortune figured Klein's annual income at $8.5 million. In the mid-1970s, he had created a designer-jeans craze by putting his name on the back pocket. Klein's design assistant at the time, Jeffrey Banks, has claimed credit for the logo garments, stating that he had the logo from a press folder silkscreened onto the sleeve of a brown T-shirt as a present for Klein. The gift was assumed by Schwartz to be part of the upcoming line, and similar logo shirts formed the uniform for the front-of-house staff at Klein's next catwalk show, leading to buyer demand.

In the late 1970s, the company also made attempts to set up its own fragrance and cosmetics lines, but soon withdrew from the market with big financial losses.

1980s

In the 1980s, as the designer-jeans frenzy reached its all-time high, Calvin Klein introduced a highly successful line of boxer shorts for women and a men's underwear collection which would later gross $70 million in a single year. The American market of men's underwear was changed – from one where most men's underwear was white, purchased in packs of three by a "wife, mother or girlfriend when they needed to be" to one where "the American male [cares] about the brand of something few ever see"

Growth continued through the early eighties. The licensing program, which brought in $24,000 when it was initiated in 1974 (equivalent to $125,943 in 2020), had royalty income of $7.3 million ten years later (equivalent to $18.18 million in 2022). That year, worldwide retail sales were estimated at more than $60 million (equivalent to $1494.62 million in 2022). Klein's clothes were sold through 12,000 stores in the United States and were available in six other countries through licensing deals, namely Canada, the United Kingdom, Ireland, Australia, New Zealand, and Japan. His annual income passed $12 million (equivalent to $29.89 million in 2022).

Financial problems increased pressure from all sides, disagreements with the licensee of the menswear line and its disappointing sales as well as an enormous employee turnover both within Calvin Klein and its licensing partners led to the first rumors that Calvin Klein Industries, as the company had been known by then, was up for sale. And indeed, in late 1987, it was said that the sale of the company to Triangle Industries, a container manufacturer, had only failed because of the crashing stock market.

1990s

Although the company almost faced bankruptcy in 1992, Calvin Klein managed to regain and increase the profitability of his empire throughout the later 1990s, mainly through the success of its highly popular underwear and fragrance lines, as well as the ck sportswear line. During his 1990–1995 stint as Calvin Klein's head of menswear design, John Varvatos pioneered a type of men's underwear called boxer briefs, a hybrid of boxer shorts and briefs. Made famous by a series of 1992 print ads featuring Mark "Marky Mark" Wahlberg, they have been called "one of the greatest apparel revolutions of the century."

Klein was named "America's Best Designer" for his minimalist all-American designs in 1993, and it came as a surprise in 1999 when it was announced that CKI was again up for sale. Planning to expand its business, the company had been approached by two luxury goods companies, LVMH and Pinault Printemps Redoute, to join Calvin Klein, but nothing resulted. Other potentials like Tommy Hilfiger Corp. and Italy's Holding di Partecipazioni proved to be similar disappointments because of CKI's steep price tag of supposedly $1 billion. After seven months and no potential buyer, Klein announced that his empire was not on the market anymore. The company would never manage to go public, which had supposedly been Klein's plan once.

2002–present: Acquisition by Phillips van Heusen

In mid-December 2002, Calvin Klein Inc. (CKI) was sold to Phillips Van Heusen Corp (PVH), whose then CEO Bruce Klatskywas the driving force behind the deal, for about $400 million in cash, $30 million in stock as well as licensing rights and royalties linked to revenues over the following 15 years that were estimated at $200 to $300 million. The sale also included an ongoing personal financial incentive for Klein based on future sales of the Calvin Klein brand.

PVH outbid VF Corp., the maker of Lee and Wrangler jeans, which had also been interested in the jeans, underwear and swimwear business of CK that had been controlled by Warnaco Group, maker of Speedo swimwear in the US, since 1997. The deal with PVH did not include these businesses, and they remained with Warnaco. Unable to pay debts from acquisitions and licensing agreements and due to bad publicity by a later dismissed lawsuit with Calvin Klein over selling license products to retailers other than agreed upon with Calvin Klein, Warnaco had filed for chapter 11 protection in mid-2001 but eventually emerged from bankruptcy in February 2003.

The transaction between Calvin Klein and PVH was financially supported by Apax Partners Inc., a New York private equity firm, which is said to have made a $250 million equity investment in PVH convertible preferred stock, as well as a $125 million, two-year secured note, all in exchange for seats on the board of PVH.

CKI thus became a wholly owned subsidiary of PVH. In the beginning, Klein himself, who was included as a person in the 15-year contract he had signed with PVH, remained creative head of the collections but then continued as an advisor (consulting creative director) to the new company from 2003 on and has since been more withdrawn from the business. Barry K. Schwartz was said to concentrate on his role as chairman of the New York Racing Association, a horse-racing club. The current President and COO of the CKI division within PVH are Tom Murry, who had filled this position already before the acquisition.

Upon the acquisition of Calvin Klein, Phillips-Van Heusen announced plans of launching a new men's sportswear collection that rivals Ralph Lauren's collection. This line is produced by Van Heusen.

With the fall 2006 Collection runway presentations in New York City, CKI inaugurated an 8,600 sq ft (800 m^2) showroom space that can seat up to 600 people on the ground floor of 205 West 39th Street, in Times Square South where Calvin Klein has been headquartered since 1978.

In a 2010 report, PVH, who manages the ready-to-wear activities, had estimated sales of €4.6 billion of Calvin Klein products .In February 2013, Warnaco Group was acquired by PVH which united Calvin Klein formal, underwear, jeans and sportswear lines.

In 2020, PVH announced that as part of their animal welfare policy, the company does not use exotic skins and would be banning their use in Calvin Klein collections when "our annual update of that policy is released.

PRODUCTS

The most visible brand names in the Calvin Klein portfolio include:

- Calvin Klein 205W39NYC (black label, upscaletop-end designer line)
- ck Calvin Klein (grey label, recently repositioned as bridge collection line; licensed to Warnaco Group, Inc. through at least 2044. PVH acquired Warnaco Group in Feb 2013)
- **Calvin Klein** (white label, basic fashion better sportswear line)
- **Calvin Klein Sport** (sports version of the white label line for Macy's)
- **Calvin Klein Jeans** (denimwear line; licensed to Warnaco Group through at least 2044. PVH acquired Warnaco Group in Feb 2013)
- **Calvin Klein Home** (high end bedding, towel, bath rug and accessory collections)
- **The Khaki Collection** (youthful medium to high end bedding, towel, bath rug and accessories) discontinued in 2008
- **Calvin Klein Golf** (launched in late 2007)
- **Calvin Klein Underwear** (underwear collections; licensed to Warnaco Group through at least 2044. PVH acquired Warnaco Group in Feb 2013)
- **CK one Lifestyle brand** (fragrance, underwear, jeans -launched 2011)
- **Calvin Klein Watches + Jewelry** (watches launched in 1997, jewelry in 2004)

Fragrance

Calvin Klein has various lines of perfumes and colognes, including Obsession, CK Be, and Eternity. Until May 2005, their perfumes and the corresponding fragrance lines were maintained by Calvin Klein Cosmetics Company (CKCC), a Unilever company. Cosmetics giant Coty, Inc. of New York bought the fragrance licensing agreements from Unilever.

- **CHRISTIAN DIOR**

A French fashion designer, best known as the founder of one of the world's top fashion houses Christian Dior SE, which is now owned by parent company LVMH. His fashion houses are known all around the world, specifically "on five continents in only a decade" (Sauer).

HISTORY

Christian Dior was born in Granville, a seaside town on the coast of Normandy, France. He was the second of five children born to Maurice Dior, a wealthy fertilizer manufacturer (the family firm was Dior Frères), and his wife, formerly Madeleine Martin. He had four siblings: Raymond (father of Françoise Dior), Jacqueline, Bernard, and Catherine Dior. When Christian was about five years old, the family moved to Paris, but still returned to the Normandy coast for summer holidays.

Dior's family had hoped he would become a diplomat, but Dior was artistic and wished to be involved in art. To make money, he sold his fashion sketches outside his house for about 10 cents each. In 1928, Dior left school and received money from his father to finance a small art gallery, where he and a friend sold art by the likes of Pablo Picasso. The gallery was closed three years later, following the deaths of Dior's mother and brother, as well as financial trouble during the Great Depression that resulted in his father losing control of the family business.

From 1937, Dior was employed by the fashion designer Robert Piguet, who gave him the opportunity to design for three Piguet collections. Dior would later say that 'Robert Piguet taught me the virtues of simplicity through which true elegance must come.'[7][8] One of his original designs for Piguet, a day dress with a short, full skirt called "Cafe Anglais", was particularly well received. Whilst at Piguet, Dior worked alongside Pierre Balmain, and was succeeded as house designer by Marc Bohan – who would, in 1960, become head of design for Christian Dior Paris. Dior left Piguet when he was called up for military service.

In 1942, when Dior left the army, he joined the fashion house of Lucien Lelong, where he and Balmain were the primary designers. For the duration of World War II, Dior, as an employee of Lelong – who labored to preserve the French fashion industry during wartime for economic and artistic reasons – in attempts to preserve the fashion industry during the war, Dior designed dresses for the wives of Nazi officers and French collaborators, as did other fashion houses that remained in business during the war, including Jean Patou, Jeanne Lanvin, and Nina Ricci. His sister, Catherine (1917–2008), served as a member of the French Resistance, was captured by the Gestapo, and sent to the Ravensbrück concentration camp, where she was incarcerated until her liberation in May 1945. In 1947, he named his debut fragrance, Miss Dior in tribute to his sister.

FASHION HOUSE

In 1946 Marcel Boussac, a successful entrepreneur known as the richest man in France, invited Dior to design for Philippe et Gaston, a Paris fashion house launched in 1925. Dior refused, wishing to make a fresh start under his own name rather than reviving an old brand. On 8 December 1946, with Boussac's backing, Dior founded his fashion house. The actual name of the line of his first collection, presented on 12 February 1947, was Corolle (literally the botanical term corolla or circlet of flower petals in English), but the phrase New Look was coined for it by Carmel Snow, the editor-in-chief of Harper's Bazaar. Though called "New," it was clearly drawn from styles of the Edwardian era[15] and it merely refined and crystallized trends in skirt shape and waistline that had been burgeoning in high fashion since the late 1930s. Nonetheless, Dior's designs were more voluptuous than the boxy, fabric-conserving shapes of the recent World War II styles, influenced by the rations on fabric. He was a master at creating shapes and silhouettes; Dior is quoted as saying "I have designed flower women." His look employed fabrics lined predominantly with percale, boned, bustier-style bodices, hip padding, wasp-waisted corsets and petticoats that made his dresses flare out from the waist, giving his models a very curvaceous form.

Initially, women protested because his designs covered up their legs, which they had been unused to because of the previous limitations on fabric. There was also some backlash to Dior's designs due to the amount of fabrics used in a single dress or suit. Of the "New Look", Gabrielle "Coco" Chanel said the following, "Look how ridiculous these women are, wearing clothes by a man who doesn't know women, never had one, and dreams of being one." During one photo shoot in a Paris market, the models were attacked by female vendors over this profligacy, but opposition ceased as the wartime shortages ended.

The "New Look" revolutionized women's dress and reestablished Paris as the centre of the fashion world after World War II,[18] as well as making Dior a virtual arbiter of fashion for much of the following decade,[19] each season featuring a newly titled Dior "line," in the manner of 1947's "Corolle" line, that would then be trumpeted in the fashion press: the Envol and Cyclone/Zigzag lines in 1948, the Trompe l'Oeil and Mid-Century lines in 1949, the Vertical and Oblique lines in 1950, the Naturelle/Princesse and Longue lines in 1951, the Sinueuse and Profilée lines in 1952, the Tulipe and Vivante lines in 1953, the Muguet/Lily of the Valley line and H-Line in 1954, the A-Line and Y-Line in 1955, the Flèche/Arrow and Aimant/Magnet lines in 1956, and the Libre/Free and Fuseau/Spindle lines in 1957,[20][21] followed by successor Yves Saint Laurent's Trapeze line in 1958.

In 1955, the 19-year-old Yves Saint Laurent became Dior's design assistant. Christian Dior later met with Yves Saint Laurent's mother, Lucienne Mathieu-Saint Laurent, in 1957 to tell her that he had chosen Saint Laurent to succeed him at Dior. She said at the time she had been confused by the remark, as Dior was only 52 at the time.

AWARDS

- Dior was nominated for the 1955 Academy Award for Best Costume Design in black and white for the Terminal Station directed by Vittorio De Sica (1953).
- Dior was also nominated in 1967 for a BAFTA for Best British Costume (Colour) for the Arabesque directed by Stanley Donen (1966).
- Nominated in 1986 for his contributions to the 1985 film, Bras de fer, he was up for Best Costume Design (Meilleurs costumes) during the 11th Cesar Awards.

PRODUCTS

- Bags
- Acessories

AN OVERVIEW OF INDIAN FASHION DESIGNERS

- **MANISH MALHOTRA**

Manish Malhotra (born December 5, 1966) is an Indian fashion designer, couturier, costume stylist, entrepreneur, filmmaker, revivalist based in Mumbai, India.

The founder of the eponymous label, Manish Malhotra, has been deeply entrenched in the twin worlds of fashion and film for the past three decades. He has styled and designed for more than thousands of movies and won numerous awards. He is known for redefining and modernizing how actors look in Indian movies and reviving some of the country's forgotten crafts.

The recipient of several awards rose to prominence for his elaborate work in cinema with Bollywood, Telugu, Tamil, Hollywood, Television, and the Fashion industry.

Manish Malhotra became famous for his outlook on the importance of costumes in films, often becoming a part of the narration and script reading process to develop costumes for films.

He has also been felicitated with Priyadarshini Memorial Award for his contribution to the fashion industry. Filmfare introduced the 'best costume design' award in 1996 to acknowledge Manish Malhotra for his styling and designing work in the film 'Rangeela' released in 1995.

Since 2018 Manish has launched four other new verticals - Manish Malhotra Beauty, Manish Malhotra Jewellery, a Film Production company, and Home decor.

He is set to make his directorial debut with a musical love story, set in the backdrop of the partition, produced by Dharma Productions.

Accoladed as a pioneer in the Indian design space, Manish Malhotra's areas of creativity span the broad spheres of cinema, design, styling, diffusion, timeless bridal couture, jewelry, beauty, film direction, Virtual Store, and now

Tech with his recent launch of NFT's in the blockchainbusiness.

CARRIER

Stylist and designer

Manish Malhotra made his costume designing debut, in 1990, with the movie Swarg starring Govinda, Rajesh Khanna, and Juhi Chawla.

The same year his gateway to the fashion industry opened when Rakesh Sreshtha, a photographer, introduced him to the late Sridevi to style her photoshoot looks.

His creative process as a costume stylist began with script readings – an unheard-of practice in Hindi films then. He believed that costume was an integral part of visual storytelling to make the characters more relatable to the audience.

Manish was known to be the first costume stylist and designer to view the film as a whole. He advised the actresses and filmmakers on aspects where the character's look would just be a subset of the overall creative input, lending the costume looks their due credit.

In 1993, he designed a complete look for Sridevi's character in Mahesh Bhatt's Gumrah.

The film industry designer said it was during the 1993's Telugu thriller Govinda Govinda when Ram Gopal Varma first noticed his designs for Sridevi and reached out to him for Rangeela (1995).

Rangeela was a career-changing experience for him as the success of the film and the popularity of the fashion trends the movie established saw Filmfare Awards introduce a new category for costume designing, with Malhotra being the first recipient.

Malhotra was credited for his modern and minimal yet impactful costume styling - be it the chiffon sarees in "Hai Rama," the tangerine skater dress and the printed dress on a white base in "Tanha Tanha", pleated skirts, and boyfriend shorts in "Rangeela Re" or the Chaplinesque look in "Kya Kare Kya Na Kare". Her casual style - from co-ords, skater dresses, leotards with scarves to oversized shirts, high-waist jeans with figure-hugging tees, and wool berets- is one of the main talking points of this film.

In 1997, Manish was offered a styling and designing project for Yash Raj Chopra'sDil Toh Pagal Hai. The film depicts the love lives of the dancers in a musical dance troupe while introducing stylish athleisure wear, sheer traditional outfits, and minimal styling to Hindi Cinema.

From bicycle shorts, sports bras, wrist bands on Karisma Kapoor to Madhuri Dixit's sheer suit sets in lace and chiffon symbolic of her coy nature; made most Indian women line up at the shops for copies.

The costumes and styling of Karan Johar'sKuch Kuch Hota Hai created an absolute frenzy back in 1998, courtesy of the man behind the fashion department, Manish Malhotra, for which he won 7 individual category awards.

The DKNY tracksuits, activewear, uber-casual sweatshirts, logo tees, and denim adorned by Kajol or minimal dress to co-ords layered with oversized outerwear and the high-octane mini dress worn by Rani Mukerji, Kajol in the latter half of the film was seen draped in sheer sarees with a hint of lace, or solid versions with an emphasis on the blouse; pastel hues and layering kurtas with sleek trousers which came to the forefront, bringing with them a timeless appeal. The off-route orange and beige lehenga as opposed to the go-to bridal red iteration. From athleisure, casual to bridal looks, Manish garnered recognition to create an array of fashion-forward looks now omnipresent and trendsetting.

In 1999, Karan Johar offered Manish Malhotra to design for the multi-starrer family drama Kabhi Khushi Kabhie Gham..., Kareena Kapoor's look in the film was styled by Manish, which cemented her position as a 'true style icon' and set the entire tone for the film.

The red coordinated set of sequin top with bell-bottom pants from 'You Are My Soniya', The pastel pink choli-pants paired with an asymmetrical cut bodice from 'Bole Chudiyan,' The yellow strapless top with the sunflower choker and ombre sunglasses, Shimmer crop tops, mini-skirts, leather pants, jackets and scarves, fur collars. Manish Malhotra's styling in the film K3G is perceived to be timeless and relevant, and inspirational for every generation.

2001 was when he won the first-ever IIFA Best Costume award for the musical romantic drama Mohabbatein.

In 2003, for Kal Ho Naa Ho, Manish worked his skills on the storyline based on NRI people. Preity Zinta's statement pieces included scarves, trench coats, halter dresses (the red one), sweaters, slip dresses, flared pants, one-Shoulder trend —relevant to the era and character. Shah Rukh Khan and Saif Ali Khan's embroidered kurtas and Preity's blue "Maahi Ve" lehenga, saw them romancing with twinning colours.

The same year, he designed wedding outfits for the actress Karishma Kapoor subsequently leading to inquiries from high-profile clientele like the Raheja Builders and many more.

2004, Manish Malhotra generated noise for styling Sushmita Sen in the films Main Hoon Na with flowy chiffon sarees, vibrant colors, and prints.

Manish is known for making women feel sultry in sarees.

In 2006, Malhotra styled the entire cast of Johar's ensemble musical romantic drama Kabhi Alvida Naa Kehna. Set in New York City, the film revolved around affluent NRI's, thus providing Malhotra to flex his styling skills to the highest level. The costumes, styling and overall looks of the characters in the film proved to be highly popular and acclaimed.

In 2007, Manish Malhotra styled Kareena Kapoor's character Geet in the film Jab We Met. The movie saw the rise of harem pants paired with long t-shirts, phulkari scarves, corset tops (with the popular red skirt), and hoop earrings with short kurtas.

In 2008, Manish Malhotra was praised for Priyanka Chopra Jonas's look in the movie Dostana. The vibe of the film was cool chic, and so were the costumes. It saw her shimmering golden swimsuit and her Desi Girl's classic silver saree with a sensuous blouse launched many versions of the same.

Manish Malhotra styled and designed Deepika Padukone's looks for 'Yeh jawaani hai Diwani' in 2012. The electric blue saree with a black shimmer blouse, her form-fitting kurtas with plunging necklines, low waist lehengas with short blouses, or floral dresses paired with sweaters and denim jackets, Naina Talwar's outfits received a lot of attention and praise.

His body of work of over 1000 films and designing innumerable looks for actors including Rekha Ji, Sridevi, Raveena Tandon, Kajol, Raveena Tandon, Aishwarya Rai Bachchan, Sushmita Sen to the generation of Ameesha Patel, Kareena Kapoor Khan, Deepika Padukone, Katrina Kaif, Alia Bhatt, Janhvi Kapoor, Sara Ali Khan, Ananya Pandey and many others. Famous figures like Nita Ambani, Isha Piramal, Shloka Ambani and Radhika Merchant of the Ambani family also have embraced Malhotra's dresses and outfits in several occasions. Manish has been telling stories through all his creations for three decades now.

The veteran was bestowed with the Filmfare Award for 30 years of outstanding contribution in Bollywood fashion.

The Bollywood designer became a household name because of the remembrance of the outfits he created, such as Priyanka Chopra's look in Desi Girl, a gold saree paired with a bralette, Kareena Kapoor's recognized outfits from Kabhi Khushi Kabhi Gham, Deepika Padukone's saree in Yeh Jawani hai Diwani, Kajol's net and chiffon sarees in 'Kabhi Khushi Kabhi Gum', Rani Mukerji, Preity Zinta, Jaya Bachchan and Kirron Kher's winter coats, dresses and sarees in Kal Ho Naa Ho and Kabhi Alvida Naa Kehna, to new age actors Whether it's Janhvi (Kapoor) for 'Dhadak', Sara (Ali Khan) for 'Simmba', Ananya and Tara for 'Student of the Year 2'.

Manish has styled several actors like Shah Rukh Khan in several films, including 'Om Shanti Om,' 'Happy New Year,' 'My Name is Khan', Saif Ali Khan in Kal Ho Naa Ho, Amitabh Bachchan and Abhishek Bachchan in Kabhi Alvida Naa Kehna, Ranbir Kapoor, Ranveer Singh, Varun Dhawan, Siddharth Malhotra, Imran Khan, and many others.

The visionary, revivalist, designer continues to accolade with many prestigious awards to date.

Entrepreneur:

His label "Manish Malhotra" is synonymous with opulent, contemporary, and larger-than-life glamour Indian wear.

In 1999, he collaborated with his friends, the industrialist's Kajal Anand, Yash, and Avanti Birla for a brief period to design collections for their store, Reverie.

Manish Malhotra tied up with Sheetal Design Studio and set up a workshop there. He virtually became a face of the Sheetal Design Studio, and exclusively retailed out of their store at Bombay's Grant Road for 4 years.

After claiming his position as a costume director, stylist, and Hindi Film Industry fashion designer, he launched his couture label Manish Malhotra in 2005. It offers bridal, couture, diffusion, men's wear, and bespoke collections that now retail at four Mumbai, New Delhi, and Hyderabad stores.

In 2006, Manish Malhotra teamed up with Saif Belhasa Group of Companies to open his first flagship store in Dubai that catered to Arab and Global customers. The collection portrayed a range of specially designed shelas, abhayas and jalabiyas, an amalgamation of traditional craft and modern design sensibilities to reflect the essence of his designs. The store later shut in 2017.

In 2008, he opened his first two flagship stores in Khar West, Mumbai, India.

In 2013, Manish Malhotra was the first Indian designer to have opened the largest, Indian stand-alone store sprawled over 6,000 sq.ft, located in a gorgeous haveli on Kalkadas Marg in Mehrauli, Delhi. The space reflects Malhotra's trademark opulent style with arched windows, high ceilings, and vintage chandeliers.

In 2017, Manish launched the Hyderabad store, which spreads over 15,000 sq. ft. It is located in the city's posh Jubilee Hills locality to meet the designer's grand visionary identity.

Over the years, the label's aesthetic has aimed to bring together traditional Indian craftsmanship with contemporary silhouettes like gowns with intricate gold embroidery, cigarette pants paired with long jackets for women, voluminous lehengas worn with cropped blouses, or the use of non-traditional colors like royal blue, soft pink, maroon, etc., in bridal ensembles. The label's design language is claimed to exhibit glamour and is a reflection of modern India. In 2019, many actresses wore the signature "Manish Malhotra saree" that the designer introduced in a variety of colours.

He launched his first-ever haute-couture make-up line, 'Manish Malhotra Beauty', in collaboration with My Glamm in December 2018.

2019, the celebrity couturier ventured into a new space, 'Manish Malhotra Jewellery' in partnership with heritage jeweler brand Raniwala 1881. The curation is a medley of heritage with a modern touch, much like his line of clothes, entailing an expansive range of chandbalis, danglers, studs, jhumkis, kadas, chokers, layered necklaces in a combination of uncut polkis, emeralds, diamonds, jadau, coloured stones and pearls.

Reliance Brands Limited (RBL) - part of the retail arm of billionaire Mukesh Ambani-owned Reliance Industries acquired a 40 percent stake in brand 'Manish Malhotra' (within the lifestyle space domain) to accelerate the 16-year old couture house's growth in India and across the globe. On Friday, October 15, Reliance Brands and Manish Malhotra announced a strategic partnership as part of the deal. This is the first external investment for Manish Malhotra's brand, which has been privately held by the designer so far. The brand will continue to be led by Manish Malhotra, as Managing and Creative Director after the partnership with Reliance.

COLLECTION

- Anarkali
- Lehanga
- Party wear

- **MANISH ARORA**

Indian fashion designer based in New Delhi. In early 2011, he was appointed creative director of the womenswear collection of the French fashion house Paco Rabanne,although he left the company in May 2012.

Born and brought up in Mumbai, Manish was studying, when he decided to change his career path and applied for the National Institute of Fashion Technology in New Delhi. He graduated in 1994 after winning the Best Student Award.

CARRIER

n 1997 Manish launched his own label "Manish Arora" and started retailing in India. Three years later, he participated in the first-ever India Fashion Week held in New Delhi and represented India at the Hong Kong Fashion Week.

Arora launched his second label, "Fish Fry", in 2001.This sportswear-styled line was created in association with the athletic apparel manufacturer Reebok. In 2002, Manish opened his first flagship store, Manish Arora Fish Fry, in New Delhi and in the following year opened a second store in Mumbai. Another successful showing at India Fashion Week (2003) led to a stocking deal with the fashion house Maria Luisa (Paris) and the beginning of a successful export business.

During 2004 he was awarded the Best Women's Prêt Designer at the first ever Indian Fashion Awards' 2004 held in Bombay and MC2 Diffusion Paris started representing the label for the export business. The following year Manish participated in the Miami Fashion Week in May 2005 where he was presented with the designer's choice for Best Collection Award.

He had a successful debut at the London Fashion Week in September 2005 and received an overwhelming response from the press as well as the buyers. He opened a new store at Lodhi Colony Market in New Delhi in December 2005. Arora exhibited some of his work at the Victoria & Albert Museum in London for an exhibition called "Global Local" in association with the British Council, India.

A fashion jury in a leading Indian publication Outlook designated him "Best Indian Fashion Designer" and featured him on the cover of its March 2006 issue. Manish opened his first Manish Arora franchise store in Villa Moda, Kuwait and another Manish Arora Fish Fry store at Crescent at The Qutub, New Delhi in 2006.

In 2007 the first Fish Fry for Reebok concept store opened at the Garden of Five Senses, New Delhi, and Arora teamed up with make-up and cosmetics company MAC for designing a signature collection. He has also collaborated with Swatch for a limited edition of watches. In 2008, once again, Reebok launched the 'RBK Fish Fry Collection 2008', a lifestyle range designed by Manish Arora.

"Indian by Manish Arora", a brand designed for the growing Indian market for women's wear, is licensed to another fashion company. Manish was invited to show his collection at the "Fashion in Motion" exhibition held at Victoria and Albert Museum, London in September 2007. By 2009 Manish owned four stores in India and sold his collections to more than 80 retailers worldwide. The designer has also entered into a joint venture with BIBA Apparels Pvt. Ltd. to further expand the label.

In 2012, Arora previewed his jewellery line in association with label Amrapali comprising a range of hand jewellery, neckpieces and pendants.

Some of his work was displayed at the Victoria and Albert Museum, in the Fabric of India 2014-15 Exhibition.

STYLE

Manish Arora is regarded by many as "the John Galliano of India". He is known for his psychedelic colour palette and kitsch motifs in garments that combine traditional Indian crafts like embroidery, appliqué and beading with Western silhouettes.

- **RITU BERI**

She became head of the Ready to Wear section of French fashion brand, Jean-Louis Scherrer,in March 2002.

She launched a not-for-profit organisation, The Luxury League to promote creativity and innovation in the luxury industry of India.She was appointed an advisor to the Khadi and Village Industries Commission (KVIC), a part of the Ministry of Micro, Small and Medium Enterprises, Government of India. She is also an advisor to Rishihood University.

CARRIER

In 2000, Beri became head of the French fashion house, Jean Louis Scherrer, to design their pret-a-porter collections.

Ritu Beri was awarded the Chevalier des Arts et des Lettres (Knight of the Order of Arts and Letters) by the French government in 2010.

On 9 April 2016, Beri launched two books, The Designs of A Restless Mind and The Fire of A Restless Mind.

AWARDS

- 2016 - Power Brands Hall of Fame
- 2014 - Order of Civil Merit by the Spanish government
- 2010 - Chevalier des Arts et des Lettres by the French government

- **TARUN TAHILIANI**

Tarun Tahiliani is a noted Indianfashion designer. With his wife Sailaja 'Sal' Tahiliani, he co-founded Ensemble, India's first multi-designer boutique in 1987, followed by Tahiliani Design studio in 1990. Based in Delhi, he is best known for his ability to infuse Indian craftsmanship and textile heritage with tailored silhouette. His signature is to combine traditional aesthetics with modern design. Over the years, he also became known for his bridalwear.

Of late, Tahiliani has taken on several projects in interior design. He has designed interiors for hotels (such as The Sofala, Goa), restaurants (the Aish at the Park, Hyderabad), resorts and homes, and has even begun to event design for Indian weddings.

CARRIER

On returning to India, he first joined the family business in oil-field equipments. Eventually, in 1987 he and Sailaja opened the first multi-designer boutique in India, 'Ensemble' with help of designer Rohit Khosla in Mumbai. The stored featured works of five designers Abu Jani & Sandeep Khosla, Rohit Khosla, Anuradha Mafatlal, American fashion designer Neil Bieff and label Anaya, by Anita Shivdasani and Sunita Kapoor, Anil Kapoor's wife and their own label, Ahilian. By now, he had started sketching however he was still untrained a designer, thus in 1991, he went to Fashion Institute of Technology (FIT) in New York to study designing. After his return he shifted business to Delhi. When in 1995, British heiress Jemima Khan wore one of his outfit for her wedding to Imran Khan, his work was first noticed

Today, after over 25 years, Ensemble has stores both in Mumbai and Delhi, and Tahiliani runs the chain with his sister Tina Tahiliani Parikh, who joined the business in 1990.

Tarun also worked with Save the Children India to urge the government to increase the health budget to 3 per cent ahead of the budget announcement.

- **ROHIT BAL**

Rohit Bal was born in the city of Srinagar in the Kashmir Valley of the Jammu and Kashmir state of India on 8th May, 1961 into a Kashmiri Pandit family. He graduated from Woodlands House School and then Burn Hall School in Srinagar before having to move to New Delhi with his family for being a Kashmiri Hindu during the Insurgency in Jammu and Kashmir and attending Delhi Public School, Mathura Road. Bal then received his Bachelor's degree in History from St. Stephens College, University of Delhi.He went on to study fashion at the National Institute of Fashion Technology in Delhi

CARRIER

Rohit Bal started his career with his brother Rajiv Bal in New Delhi in 1986 the Company Orchid Oversea Pvt.Ltd, and started his own first independent collection in 1990.

Bal was also chosen by the Khadi Gram Udyog, the largest handloom textile operation in Panchkula, to work with them.

Bal has designed costumes for the popular Indian game show Kaun Banega Crorepati.

Bal opened a flagship store in Delhi, as well as stores in Mumbai, Bangalore, Ahmedabad, Kolkata and Chennai. Bal has also ventured into designing jewellery.He is best known for his use of lotus and peacock motifs. He frequently uses rich fabrics like velvet, brocade and his designs are elaborate, inspired by Indian grandeur and royalty.

He has an international client base that includes Cindy Crawford, Pamela Anderson and Uma Thurman among various Indian celebrities.He is also an ambassador for Omega watches.

- **WENDELL RODRICK**

Indian fashion designer and author based in the Indian state of Goa.He was also an activist for social causes, the environment, and gay rights. In 2014, the Government of India conferred upon him its fourth-highest civilian award, the Padma Shri.

Fashion

Rodricks began his career in fashion by designing for Garden Vareli, Lakmé Cosmetics and DeBeers. When in Paris with his first portfolio in hand, he was advised to put "your country in your clothes". He launched his own label in 1989 with his first show held at the Regal Room of the Oberoi Hotel, Mumbai. His first collection consisted of twelve ensembles, with model Mehr Jesia. Out of these, only six were complete outfits. He did not have enough funds for supplying all models with shoes or bottoms for their organza tunics. Henceforth, Rodricks' work involved a wide range of fashion, from lecturing on world costume history (at SNDT Women's University) to fashion journalism and styling for international advertising campaigns.] He was the first Indian designer to be invited to IGEDO (the world's largest garment fair) in 1995; the first Indian designer to open the Dubai Fashion Week in 2001; and was invited to present at the Paris Fashion WeekPret a Porter salon in 2007. He was a fellow design member of the Fashion Design Council of India.

Rodricks was known for pioneering the idea of resort wear and for advocating eco-friendly fashion. In 2010, he revived the traditional Goan attire of the kunbisari. He convinced Pratibha Patil, Priyanka Gandhi and Sonia Gandhi to be its patrons, thus increasing the cost from a meagre Rs. 700 to more than Rs. 7000, for the benefit of the weavers. He was also a part of the khadi movement, and even promoted it at the world's largest organic fair, BioFach, at Nuremberg, Germany, in 2011 when he was invited there. In 2017, he presented a collection for plus-size women at the Lakme Fashion Week in 2017.

Rodricks dressed many over the decades. When his close friend Lisa Ray decided to get married in 2012, she chose a gown designed by him. In 2014, he paid tribute to actress Rekha at the Wills Lifestyle India Fashion Week (WIFW), on the occasion of her 60th birthday. Rodricks helped Deepika Padukone, who had been modelling with him for roughly two years then, grab her role in Om Shanti Om by recommending her to Malaika Arora, who in turn recommended her to Farah Khan in 2007. He also helped Anushka Sharma, launching her as a model in his 2007 Les Vamps Show at the Lakme Fashion Week and encouraged her to move to Mumbai when she was just 18 years old.

In 2016, he announced his retirement from his label, to concentrate on his museum. He handed over creative control to his student, Schulen Fernandes, who first worked with him in 1999.

AWARDS

- Padma Shri in 2014
- Chevalier de l'Ordre des Arts et Lettres (transl. Knight of the Order of Arts and Letters) in 2015
- Rainbow Warrior Award in 2014 by KASHISH Mumbai International Queer Film Festival

- **JJ VALAYA**

J Valaya (born 8 October 1967) is a noted Indian fashion designer and couturier from New Delhi, India. He founded the House of Valaya, a luxury fashion and lifestyle house in 1992, along with his brother TJ Singh. A founding member of Fashion Design Council of India (FDCI) and the first global brand ambassador of Crystal giant Swarovski, he has been designing for men and women, and has bridal and evening collections in addition to day-wear and ready-to-wear for over 20 years. As a fine art photographer, he released his first book, Decoded Paradox in 2011, in the same year as he also closed the day one of the Lakme Fashion Week (LFW) winter/festive 2011, debuting a fashion collection inspired by photography.

CARRIER

He trained under a pioneer in Indian fashion Rohit Khosla, before starting his own label.With his elder brother TJ (Tribhavan Jit) Singh, JJ Valaya founded The House of Valaya in 1992 with the launch of its couture label. Valaya's creative vision together with his brother's organizational abilities have been the key factors for the success of Valaya as a luxury brand.Around 2003, when he launched his pret line, he was already retailing fashion and lifestyle products under three brands: JJ Valaya, Studio Valaya and Valaya Home-Life, in which his first couture label, JJ Valaya, comprising his trousseau line, launched in 1993.The brand today encompasses Couture, Ready-to-wear, Home and a CSR prerogative, The Free Spirit Foundation (FSF).

In 2010, Valaya's collection of **ALIKA** showcased at several events in Dubai was highly acclaimed. In this collection, the storyteller in him found expression through which he narrated the story of the female musicians of India's royal courts and their romantic affairs with the princes of the land. Alika, his fall/winter range consisted of finely worked jalabiyas, kaftan saris and anarkali-churidars.Valaya has used his couture creations to tell stories that intrigue him. That's perhaps part of the reason for his fascination with India's royal history. This collection also saw the birth of his signature Alika Jacket.

In 2011, Valaya's Winter/Festive collection at Lakme Fashion Week titled **TASVEER** received positive reviews. The collection combined Valaya's twin passions: photography and fashion. The collection was inspired by the evolution of photography from black and white to sepia to hand-stained, natural and digitised images. It was an interesting journey of colours and an amazing story, told through clothes. Valaya, in one of his interviews said "It's almost like there are two personae in me: the photographer and the fashion designer. I intend to keep both alive," there was also about 10 menswear outfits that included sherwanis, bandhgalas, breeches and Nehru jackets.

In 2012, Wills India Fashion Week Valaya's collection **AZRAK** stayed true to its meaning – rare and common. The collection was inspired by West Asia and the Ottoman Empire of Turkey. His creations had juxtaposed elements of minimalism and grandeur, Western and Indian silhouettes, traditional motifs and modern drapes & feminine form. The range showcased saris, jackets, anarkalis, breeches, blouses and dresses. Showstopper Bollywood actress Kangana Ranaut was dressed in a pristine white gown teamed with traditional Indian jewellery and a rich brocade Maharaja coat. The surprise elements on the ramp were faces such as Suneet Verma, Rohit Bal, Navtej Johar, Jamie Stewart, Sumant Jayakrishnan and Navin Ansal to name a few, who were among the twelve showstoppers that took to the runway for the designer.

The year 2012 also marks 20 years of JJ Valaya's work in the fashion industry. The designer took a series of initiatives – launched a limited edition financial year calendar in Delhi. Shot by noted fashion photographer Tarun Khiwal, the April 2012 to March 2013 calendar has Valaya's close friends and "wonderfully inspired individuals".

Valaya introduced the 'Diasun', a pattern comprising two inverted 'V' and the sun motif from the JJ Valaya crest, which now comes on every garment produced by the label in some way or the other to put a stop to plagiarism and imitations of the market.

JJ Valaya is a founder member of the Board of Governors of the Fashion Design Council of India

The designer currently has around 250 embroidered workers and craftsmen working exclusively for him out of 40,000 sq ft headquarters in Delhi.

His clothes have been worn by various GCC royals and celebrities including Joseph Fiennes, Cate Blanchett, Hrithik Roshan and Kareena Kapoor.

He remains one of the biggest names in the bridal trousseau market in India, and was one of the first Indian labels to invest in sampling, research and development at their "House of Valaya" establishment at Manesar on the outskirts of Delhi

AWARDS

Founder board member of the Governing Council/ board of directors of the Fashion Design Council of India (FDCI). (1998)

CHAPTER III

FASHION PRODUCTS AND PROMOTION

INTRODUCTION

The prevailing style (as in dress) during a particular time The spring fashions are now on display.

We have four seasons in our calendar year. Spring, Summer, Fall, and Winter. Typically in the fashion world, these are combined into two seasons as Spring/Summer and Fall/Winter. Spring/Summer begins in January and ends in June. Fall/Winter picks up in July and runs through December.Seasonal clothing doesn't fall exactly into a fashion's calendar pattern. You might walk into a store during the Summer and notice that the stores are already set up with pumpkins, scarves, and sweaters. As a fashion designer, when it's mid season of Spring/Summer you should be finalizing and close to receiving your Fall/Winter collection

The main reason why you need to plan your clothing designs at least a season early is that it will take time to manufacture. You need time to design, create your tech pack, send it to your manufacturer, receive your sample, make adjustments as needed, and possibly create a second sample, before you finalize your product design so that production can begin. The whole process from start to finish can take at least six months. If you're submitting your Spring designs in January, you have already lost your window to sell that collection which leaves you with overstocked products that won't move. This is a big cost for you as it will be hard to break even at this point.

FASHION SEASON

Fashion seasons may be perplexing and even intimidating. There has been much discussion about the fashion industry shifting away from seasonal collections. Therefore we believe it is necessary to analyze why we have seasons in the first place and how they operate now.

In this article, we'll look at why there's been such a strong push for "seasonless" fashion, as well as what it implies for customers. We'll also look at some of the most popular forecasts for the end of the seasonal apparel lines and the advent of the ultra-fast-fashion. seasons as periods when the weather changed and imagined that major fashion seasons were about altering what you wore in response to the changing climate: Warmer garments in colder weather, brighter colors in the sun, and more practical designs when it's wet.

It turns out to be significantly more complicated. The seasons serve as a global metronome for the worldwide fashion business, defining the speed and time for developing, marketing, and selling new collections.

FASHION PROMOTION & FASHION COMMUNICATION

Fashion promotion is a key element of the marketing mix. The task of promotion is to communicate with customers and publicize products and services. Promotional activities such as advertising, public relations and sales promotions are used to build a brand's status, enhance perception of a brand, increase desire for products, raise awareness of what's on offer and inform consumers about benefits or services. The ultimate aim of promotion is of course is to support sales and persuade consumers to purchase.

Purposes of Fashion Promotion:

- Inform: Create awareness
- Persuade: Convince customers of benefits of the product
- Remind: Reinforces where products are available

Consumer Promotion:

- Directly to consumers
- On a national level
- By textile and manufacturing firms
- Preselling to consumers (so they ask for it)

Trade Promotion:

- Aimed within the industry
- Stresses performance of the product
- Can involve conventions and trade shows

Retail Promotion

- By a store to it's customers
- Usually on a local level
- Centered around seasons and traditional buying patterns.

Part of the Marketing Mix: Place, Product, Price, Promotion

- Promotional mix: the combination of all types of persuasive communication used by an organization to market itself and influence sales.
- Promotion mix for fashion companies: advertising, public relations and publicity, visual merchandising, and special events
- Promotion goals and objectives:

- Used to evaluate the effectiveness of the promotion
- Could include selling certain merchandise, larger sales in general, or increased market share
- Message or theme
- Specific Activities
- Should relate to goals and objectives

Timing of Activities

- How many messages to run
- How often to run them
- Length of time (weeks, month)
- Media Mix
- Newspaper, radio, etc
- Assignments of responsibility
- Specifies people and departments to create and carry out each aspect of the promotion

Budget and Expenditures

- Evaluation Method

The promotional mix

The promotional mix refers to the combination of promotional tools used by a company to promote products and services and communicate their message to consumers

Fashion promotion is indirect technique used for selling the company products targeted to attract mass audience. It is a non-personal, aiming public in general. Therefore, it is always generated enough interest in the sales field. Public attention is drawn by keeping the needs and requirements of the public through aesthetic creation of different designs. **Fashion voucher codes, 2015**, allows people to know more about these trends and it also allows them to get involved in the recent trends and fashion. The entire concept of fashion promotion is to help and develop a uniform platform to reach targeted sales.

It is also a method to understand the requirements of individual developers, designers, retailers and whole sale dealers who are involved in the textile business. It is one of the most complex industries that requires thorough understanding and knowledge of present trends, contemporary methods, and comprehensive outlook. It is considered as tough since one has to have very good understanding of the present technology, changing trends, and new developments. It also depend ever changing demands of consumers. Therefore for the people involved in the fashion promotion to be equipped with the latest updates. They should have enough knowledge to handle the issues such as sustainability, changing technologies, political issues, legal issues, copyright acts, impact of different cultures, celebrity involvement and impact on public, use of different advertisement mediums such as films, videos, and music to spice up the events organized exclusively for the business development. It is always necessary to apply all the planning and promotional techniques to real life situations along with the advertisement analysis to get better output when fashion promotion is organized. Different case studies help and assist beginners to understand the concept of fashion promotion.

FASHION ADVERTISING AND PUBLICITY

Newspaper

n. Advantages:

- Low cost for large coverage
- Geographic selectivity
- Products can be shown

n. Disadvantages:

- Wasted circulation-not targeted
- Short life-papers thrown out
- Limited or poor color reproduction

Magazines

n. Advantages:

- Longer life span of message
- Excellent quality of color and detail
- More targeted readership

n. Disadvantages:

- Limited demonstration value
- Space is expensive
- More professional preparation needed

Outdoor

n. Advantages:

- Can select geographic location
- Repetitive viewing from audience

- Minimal cost per viewing

n. Disadvantages:

- Only a short, general message
- Some wasted audience coverage
- Considered offensive by some people

Direct Mail

n. Advantages:

- Control of what is sent
- Precise selectivity of receivers
- Results can be evaluated

n. Disadvantages:

- High cost per receiver
- Hard to get mailing lists
- Consumer resistance-junk mail thrown out

- Television

n. Advantages:

- Very popular consumer medium
- Can reach large audiences
- Has sight, sound, motion

n. Disadvantages:

- High cost of time and production
- Message is fleeting
- Longer lead time needed

Web Sites

n. Advantages:

- Interactive
- Current to reflect newest trends
- Instant worldwide market access

n. Disadvantages:

- Audience limited to computer users
- People can "click off" if not easy and understandbale

WORLD FASHION

Most people in the world today wear what can be described as "world fashion," a simplified and very low-cost version of Western clothing, often a T-shirt with pants or a skirt, manufactured on a mass scale. However, there are also numerous smaller and specialized fashion industries in various parts of the world that cater to specific national, regional, ethnic, or religious markets. Examples include the design, production, and marketing of saris in India and of boubous in Senegal. These industries operate in parallel with the global fashion industry on a minor and localized scale.

One significant development in the field of ethno-religious dress was widespread adoption of the hijab (religiously appropriate attire) among Muslim women not only in the Middle East but throughout the Islamic world in the early 21st century. With millions of Muslim women living in numerous countries worldwide, veiling norms and styles are myriad. For some, veiling can mean a withdrawal from the vicissitudes of fashion altogether. Other women, including those for whom modest garments are obligatory in public, may wear fashionable European styles underneath their more conservative street attire. Still others have sought looks that are themselves both chic and modest. At the beginning of the 21st century the international market for modest fashions was growing. Muslim and non-Muslim designers produced a widening selection of appropriate and stylish looks, and numerous fashion blogs and magazines targeting Muslim women became available. Some designers and manufacturers confronted not only the aesthetics of modest attire but also the practical challenges associated with conservative dress, as seen in efforts to produce modest yet effective swimwear and sportswear for Muslims.

FASHION SHOWS

Fashion designers and manufacturers promote their clothes not only to retailers (such as fashion buyers) but also to the media (fashion journalists) and directly to customers. Already in the late 19th century, Paris couture houses began to offer their clients private viewings of the latest fashions. By the early 20th century, not only couture houses but also department stores regularly put on fashion shows with professional models. In imitation of Parisian couturiers, ready-to-wear designers in other countries also began mounting fashion shows for an audience that combined private clients, journalists, and buyers. In the late 20th and early 21st centuries, fashion shows became more elaborate and theatrical, were held in larger venues with specially constructed elevated runways ("catwalks") for the models, and played an increasingly prominent role in the presentation of new fashions.

A fashion show (French défilé de mode) is an event put on by a fashion designer to showcase their upcoming line of clothing and/or accessories during Fashion Week. Fashion shows debut every season, particularly the Spring/Summer and Fall/Winter seasons.

In a typical fashion show, models walk the catwalk dressed in the clothing created by the designer. Clothing is illuminated on the catwalk using various forms of lighting and special effects. The order in which each model walks out, wearing a specific outfit, is usually planned in accordance with the statement that the designer wants to make about their collection. It is then up to the audience to not only try to understand what the designer is trying to say, but to also visually deconstruct each outfit and try to appreciate the detail and craftsmanship of every single piece.

Occasionally, fashion shows take the form of installations, where the models are static, standing or sitting in a constructed environment. A wide range of contemporary designers tend to produce their shows as theatrical productions with elaborate sets and added elements such as live music or a variety of technological components like holograms

By the early 21st century, fashion shows were a regular part of the fashion calendar. The couture shows, held twice a year in Paris (in January and July) by the official syndicate of couture designers (comprising the most exclusive and expensive fashion houses), present outfits that might be ordered by potential clients but which often are intended more to showcase the designers' ideas about fashion trends and brand image. Ready-to-wear fashion shows, separately presenting both women's and men's wear, are held during spring and fall "Fashion Weeks," of which the most important take place in Paris, Milan, New York, and London. However, there are literally dozens of other Fashion Weeks internationally—from Tokyo to São Paolo. These shows, of much greater commercial importance than the couture shows, are aimed primarily at fashion journalists and at buyers for department stores, wholesalers, and other major markets. Extensively covered in the media, fashion shows both reflect and advance the direction of fashion change. Photographs and videos of fashion shows are instantaneously transmitted to mass-market producers who produce inexpensive clothing copied from or inspired by the runway designs.

TYPES OF FASHION SHOW

There are major 6 types of fashion shows as described below:

- The Formal Runway Fashion Show.
- The Production Fashion Show.
- The Informal Fashion Show.
- The Designer Fashion Show.
- The Charity Fashion Show.
- The Sponsored Fashion Show.

FASHION SYSTEM

The fashion industry forms part of a larger social and cultural phenomenon known as the "fashion system," a concept that embraces not only the business of fashion but also the art and craft of fashion, and not only production but also consumption. The fashion designer is an important factor, but so also is the individual consumer who chooses, buys, and wears clothes, as well as the language and imagery that contribute to how consumers think about fashion. The fashion system involves all the factors that are involved in the entire process of fashion change. Some factors are intrinsic to fashion, which involves variation for the sake of novelty (e.g., when hemlines have been low for a while, they will rise). Other factors are external (e.g., major historical events such as wars, revolutions, economic booms or busts, and the feminist movement). Individual trendsetters (e.g., Madonna and Diana, princess of Wales) also play a role, as do changes in lifestyle (e.g., new sports, as when skateboarding was introduced in the 1960s) and music (e.g., rock and roll, hip-hop). Fashion is a complex social phenomenon, involving sometimes conflicting motives, such as creating an individual identity and being part of a group, emulating fashion leaders and rebelling against conformity. The fashion industry thrives by being diverse and flexible enough to gratify any consumer's desire to embrace or even to reject fashionability, however that term might be defined.

Sustainable fashion (also known as eco-fashion) is a movement and process of fostering change to fashion products and the fashion system towards greater ecological integrity and social justice.Sustainable fashion concerns more than just addressing fashion textiles or products. It addresses the entire manner in which clothing is produced, who produces it, and how long the life span of a product is before it reaches the landfill. This sustainable movement combats the large carbon footprint that the fashion industry and fast fashion have created by reducing greenhouse gas emissions.Reducing the environmental impact of fashion can combat air pollution, water pollution and overall climate change that could possibly prevent millions of premature deaths over the next century.Sustainable fashion deals with considering fashion from the perspective of a variety of stakeholders ranging from contemporary producers and consumers of clothes, to future producers and consumers.In 2020, it was found that an approach of voluntarily self-directed reform of textile manufacturingsupply chains to substantially reduce the environmental impact of fashion by large companies themselves has failed.Measures to reform fashion towards sustainability beyond marketing campaigns of greenwashing may need to involve policies for the creation and enforcement of standardized certificates along with related import control and subsidy-and eco-tariffs-like interventions.

SALES PROMOTION METHODS / STRATEGIES

Sales promotion letters, catalogues, point of purchase displays, customer service programmes, demonstrations, free samples, discounts, contests, sweepstakes, premiums and c Sales promotion is needed to attract new customers, to hold present customers, to counteract competition, and to take advantage of opportunities that are revealed by market research. Methods used in sales promotion include coupons, samples, premiums, point-of-purchase (POP) displays, contests, rebates, and sweepstakes.oupons are the commonly employed methods of sales promotion.

1. Free Sampling – Consumer gets one sample free, after their trial and then could decide whether to buy or not, this helps in boosting sales.

2. Offer of Price discounts/price deals – A temporary or seasonal reduction in the price, such as flat 50% off, is a good technique of attracting customers.

3. Money back and Rebates – Consumers are offered money back if the receipt and barcode are mailed to the producer.

4. Loyal customers Reward Points – Consumers collect points, miles, or credits for purchases, and redeem them for rewards, gifts or money.

5. Price-pack/Bonus packs offers – The packaging offers a consumer a certain percentage more of the product for the same price for instance, '25 percent extra', '10% extra', is seen mostly on goods. In yet another type of deal a customer is offered two products for the price of one.

In this scenario, bonus pack is disguised as a gain because buyers believe that they are obtaining a free product, though bonus pack is often wasted and is viewed as a "loss" for the consumer as the customer may not want the free product that came along with the purchase.

6. Gift Coupons or cash back coupons – coupons have become a standard mechanism for sales promotions. Many times the discount coupon issued can be redeemed on the next purchase only.

7. Mobile couponing – Coupons are available on a mobile phone. Consumers show the offer on a mobile phone to a salesperson for redemption.

8. Loss leader policy – the price of a popular product is temporarily reduced below cost in order to stimulate other profitable sales.

9. Free-standing insert (FSI) – A coupon booklet is inserted into the local newspaper for delivery, though it may not give the real benefit as mostly customers do not carefully see the pamphlets or stickers in the newspaper.

10. Attaching a small sample in the leading newspapers – especially on weekends or holidays, many companies stick their free samples such as a shampoo pouch as a sales promotion gimmick. In fact this gets noticed and the consumer feels happy on receiving a small gift like this.

STRATERGIES

1. Dump bin – this is a very popular method with big stores or Big Bazarr where bins full of products dumped inside are kept at various strategic places in order to attract attention.

2. Aisle interrupter – A sign is put up which juts into the aisle from the shelf.

3. Dangler – in order to make a customer take notice, a sign is hanged that sways, every time when a consumer walks by it.

4. Glorifier – A small stage is usually built that elevates a product above other products and glorifies it.

5. Wobbler – it is a sign that jiggles or wobbles and makes the kids, in particular, feel very good about it. Many big departmental stores keep it as a sales promotion gimmick.

6. Lipstick Board – Aboard is built on which messages are written in crayon. This also is an eye catcher and attracts attention.

7. Necker coupon – A coupon placed on the 'neck' of a bottle indicating that the particular brand or a particular size has a scheme on it.

Trade Sales Promotion Techniques:

1. Trade contest – A contest is organized with an intention to reward retailers who have sold big quantity of the product.

2. Offering Trade discounts – These are payments to distribution channel members for performing a particular function or achieving a certain target.

3. Trade credit period – a bigger trade credit period is offered to the most loyal and big dealer as an incentive.

4. Point-of-purchase displays – this technique is used to create the urge of "impulse" buying and selling the product on the spot.

5. Training programs – dealer employees are trained in selling the product and usually the training programme is kept at attractive destinations.

6. Push money or extra commission – it is also known as "spiffs" wherein extra commission is paid to retail employees to push products.

7. Trade allowances – this refers to short term incentive offered to induce a retailer to stock up on a product.

MEDIA AND MARKETING

Media of all kinds are essential to the marketing of fashion. The first dedicated fashion magazines appeared in England and France in the late 18th century. In the 19th century, fashion magazines—such as the French *La Mode Illustrée*, the British *Lady's Realm*, and the American Godey's Lady's Book—proliferated and flourished. Featuring articles, hand-coloured illustrations (known as fashion plates), and advertisements, fashion magazines—together with other developments such as the sewing machine, department stores, and ready-to-wear clothing produced in standard sizes—played a significant role in promoting the democratization of fashion in the modern era. The development of effective and inexpensive methods of reproducing photographs in print media in the early 20th century led to the rise of fashion photography and of heavily illustrated fashion magazines such as Vogue. Magazine advertising rapidly became a principal marketing tool for the fashion industry.

The creation of cinema newsreels—short motion pictures of current events—and the rise of television made it possible for people all over the world to see fashion shows and to imitate the fashionable clothing worn by celebrities. The dominance of visual media continued in the Internet age, with fashion blogs emerging as an increasingly important means of disseminating fashion information. Red-carpet events such as awards ceremonies provide an opportunity for celebrities to be photographed wearing designer fashions, thus providing valuable publicity to the designers

CHAPTER IV

FASHION RETAILING

INTRODUCTION

Once the clothes have been designed and manufactured, they need to be sold. But how are clothes to get from the manufacturer to the customer? The business of buying clothes from manufacturers and selling them to customers is known as retail. Retailers make initial purchases for resale three to six months before the customer is able to buy the clothes in-store.

The fashion industry encompasses anything sold in a fashion retail store, which may (or may not) have a recognizable brand name. Fashion designers are both product managers and innovators; they might work on a freelance or an independent basis or as part of a larger design team, such as in a retail business or within the supply chain at a manufacturer's or agent's headquarters. But the business of fashion is not built on the design function alone: areas such as forecasting, product development, manufacturing, retailing, marketing, branding and promotion combine to create a multi-billion dollar industry that employs millions worldwide. Much like the products and designs that are created, each function within this vast industry is unique. Even at the end of a major global recession, new markets continue to open up in the fashion industry because customers still want to grab a bargain, purchase something unique to wear or be seen wearing the latest trends. Fashion design and product development adds value to a retailer or fashion brand's business. However, the industry needs innovation, generated at the same rate as product consumption, or it will become stale; the fashion industry is one that plans for its products to become obsolete at the end of each season

The fashion business continues to evolve as retailers create new roles within the industry; buyers and merchandisers, product developers, sourcing managers, textile and fabric technologists are some of the industry's key roles. All of this means that for today's graduates there are many opportunities for varied career paths in the fashion business; all over the world and within different types of organization. The speed of this evolution has highlighted a number of emerging, important, considerations for the industry, including issues surrounding sustainability and ethics. The appetite for fast fashion set by certain brands is yet to slow down, as too is consumer enthusiasm for designer goods and branded products within the luxury goods sector. These consumer trends have emerged in the last decade and look set to continue in the foreseeable future. The business of fashion might be viewed as a critical path and each milestone in it, from concept to customer, is specifically designed to add value to the product. The key stages in this critical path are:

- Concept, trend and idea generation
- Design strategy
- Design and product development
- Retail strategy
- Fabric development
- Sampling × Range planning
- Sourcing strategy
- Production
- Shipping
- Distribution
- Promotion
- Sales
- Customer reaction

FASHION RETAILING

Fashion marketing is the process of managing the flow of merchandise from the initial selection of designs to be produced to the presentation of products to retail customers, with the goal of maximizing a company's sales and profitability. Successful fashion marketing depends on understanding consumer desire and responding with appropriate products. Marketers use sales tracking data, attention to media coverage, focus groups, and other means of ascertaining consumer preferences to provide feedback to designers and manufacturers about the type and quantity of goods to be produced. Marketers are thus responsible for identifying and defining a fashion producer's target customers and for responding to the preferences of those customers.

Different retailers will either elect to buy branded products or develop own-label products; the larger retailers tend to have a mixture of the two. It is important to distinguish between these strategies for the purposes of range planning, which we discuss in more detail later in the chapter. The designer has a crucial role to develop the right products at the right price. It is essential that fashion retailers employ and train designers with the ability to understand the advantages of adding value at the product development stages. This applies to all segments of the market. It is equally important to be prepared to change the process and adapt it to the ever-changing nature of the market. Designers should have the ability and confi dence to interact with buyers and merchandisers and be capable of using appropriate skills to justify their ideas for design direction and trends – this is a key dynamic in the fashion retailing sector.

SCOPE AND FUNCTIONS

Marketing operates at both the wholesale and retail levels. Companies that do not sell their own products at retail must place those products at wholesale prices in the hands of retailers, such as boutiques, department stores, and online sales companies. They use fashion shows, catalogs, and a sales force armed with sample products to find a close fit between the manufacturer's products and the retailer's customers. Marketers for companies that do sell their own products at retail are primarily concerned with matching products to their own customer base. At both the wholesale and the retail level, marketing also involves promotional activities such as print and other media advertising aimed at establishing brand recognition and brand reputation for diverse characteristics such as quality, low price, or trendiness.

Closely related to marketing is merchandising, which attempts to maximize sales and profitability by inducing consumers to buy a company's products. In the standard definition of the term, merchandising involves selling the right product, at the right price, at the right time and place, to the right customers. Fashion merchandisers must thus utilize marketers' information about customer preferences as the basis for decisions about such things as stocking appropriate merchandise in adequate but not excessive quantities, offering items for sale at attractive but still profitable prices, and discounting overstocked goods. Merchandising also involves presenting goods attractively and accessibly through the use of store windows, in-store displays, and special promotional events. Merchandising specialists must be able to respond to surges in demand by rapidly acquiring new stocks of the favoured product. An inventory-tracking computer program in a department store in London, for example, can trigger an automatic order to a production facility in Shanghai for a certain quantity of garments of a specified type and size to be delivered in a matter of days.

By the early 21st century the Internet had become an increasingly important retail outlet, creating new challenges (e.g., the inability for customers to try on clothes prior to purchase, the need for facilities designed to handle clothing returns and exchanges) and opening up new opportunities for merchandisers (e.g., the ability to provide customers with shopping opportunities 24 hours per day, affording access to rural customers). In an era of increasingly diverse shopping options for retail customers and of intense price competition among retailers, merchandising has emerged as one of the cornerstones of the modern fashion industry

TYPES OF STORES

- **Franchises**
- **Online store**
- **Specialty store**
- **Designer outlet**

- **Retail stores**
- **Department stores**
- **Branch stores**
- **Chain stores**
- **Discount stores**
- **Specialty stores**
- **Franchises**
- **Mail-order**
- **Telecommunication**

ONLINE RETAIL

Advances in technology have contributed to the huge growth in online retail, which enables consumers to shop 24/7. The advent of e-tailing has enabled brands to establish a global presence and create yet another competitive edge, a strategy that many fashion brands are now striving for in order to grow market share and increase brand equity.

DESIGNER OUTLETS

In recent years there has been a big increase in the number of large-scale retail outlets, which originated in the USA and have spread to Europe and Asia. Some of these outlet malls are used by designers to distribute out-of-season goods and excess stock. Brands such as Hugo Boss, Jil Sander, Ralph Lauren and DKNY are just some of the names that use this retail method to generate lucrative sales revenue. UK company McArthurGlen is one of the largest owners and leasing agents of such designer outlets, with a number of entire outlet villages throughout the UK and Europe.

POP-UP SHOPS

Pop-up shops, also known as 'guerilla' stores, have increased in popularity over recent years. The concept of the pop-up store is to trial new or well-known brands within a temporary shop outlet. In times of recession they have proved to be a winning low-risk format for many brands

SPECIALITY STORE

Specialty stores: Retailers that sell limited classifications of merchandise.

- Franchise stores
- Boutiques

FRANCHISES

A franchise strategy is often used by retailers who wish to internationalize because it involves low investment: the franchisee has the relevant local knowledge and invests in buying the stock, staffi ng the store and paying the rent. It means the franchisee can trade under a recognizable, well-known brand and benefi t from national or international advertising campaigns. This strategy is often used by so-called niche retailers, such as the Body Shop, Tie Rack and Accessorize. Licensing A good way for a brand to promote and expand is by selling licences to use its brand name and manufacture products; it is a market penetration technique used by many designer brands. However, it is important to monitor and police the products to ensure they remain true to the brand image. Burberry famously fell foul of over-licensing its products, most notably in Asia, and had to then carry out a costly and timeconsuming repositioning strategy

BOUTIQUE

Small, stand-alone shops or areas within larger stores that sell unusual, limited quantity apparel, accessories, or decorative items

A boutique shop is actually a specialized type of retail store. It is distinct from other retail businesses based on its more limited size, scope and inventory. When operating a retail business, it is important to understand distinct attributes, and relative strengths and weaknesses.

Business Size

One of the most significant differences between a conventional retail store and the boutique industry is the actual size of the store, according to Hello Love. A boutique is relatively small compared with a big-box retailer or general merchandise retailer. Boutiques commonly occupy small spaces in enclosed malls or in strip plazas. They are rarely stand-alone operations. In contrast, larger retail chain stores have more flexibility in location and have more space in which to sell.

Inventory Levels

Small business boutiques are also characterized by limited product variety, according to Scrapability. Variety is the amount of product categories in which you sell. Many general merchandise retailers have wide variety. Discounters Target and Wal-Mart have several product departments, for instance. A boutique specializes in a vary limited number of product or service categories. A specialty purse or hat shop might only sell that one type of product, for instance. Boutiques do often have deep assortments of that one product relative to larger retailers, however, which allows customers more choices.

Company vs. Product Passion

Though company owners, managers and employees can have passion for the company or product in any type of retailer, a boutique is often a store that evolves out of a founder's product passion. A broad-based retailer is often started by someone who desires to go into business to pursue entrepreneurial dreams. A boutique founder often crafts or orders niche goods and uses the boutique as an outlet to convert the passion into a profitable business.

Product Types

While you can create a boutique under many product categories, fashion and apparel retailers tend to most often select this store format. Companies that sell mass-merchandised goods usually want or need more floor space. Category specialists are large retailers that have expertise in product categories, but they have larger spaces and more assortment than boutiques. A boutique works well in fashion or apparel because higher-end buyers often want customized or one-of-a-kind fashions.

CHAIN STORE

A **chain store** or **retail chain** is a retail outlet in which several locations share a brand, central management, and standardized business practices. They have come to dominate the retail and dining markets, and many service categories, in many parts of the world. A franchise retail establishment is one form of chain store. In 2005, the world's largest retail chain, Walmart, became the world's largest corporation based on gross sales

DEPARTMENT STORE

A **department store** is a retail establishment offering a wide range of consumer goods in different areas of the store, each area ("department") specializing in a product category. In modern major cities, the department store made a dramatic appearance in the middle of the 19th century, and permanently reshaped shopping habits, and the definition of service and luxury. Similar developments were under way in London (with Whiteleys), in Paris (Le Bon Marché) and in New York (Stewart's)

Today, departments often include the following: clothing, cosmetics, do it yourself, furniture, gardening, hardware, home appliances, houseware, paint, sporting goods, toiletries, and toys. Additionally, other lines of products such as food, books, jewellery, electronics, stationery, photographic equipment, baby products, and products for pets are sometimes included. Customers generally check out near the front of the store in discount department stores, while high-end traditional department stores include sales counters within each department. Some stores are one of many within a larger retail chain, while others are independent retailers.

Since the 1980s, they have come under heavy pressure from discounters, and have come under even heavier pressure from e-commerce sites since 2010.

Types of Departmental Stores

These are some of the primary types of departmental stores that can be found in a city.

Discount Stores

Discount department stores are usually **retailer chains** such as **Walmart** that feature products at a lower price than the market price. They provide a large range of sections and discounts on buying a bulk quantity of goods.

Off Price Stores

These are departmental stores usually owned by a product brand or a conglomerate of product brands. In these stores, a consumer gains access to discounted products of a particular brand as they are buying directly from the manufacturer. Other features of such stores are end of season products, overproduced products, etc.

Outlet Stores

These are smaller departmental stores owned by a single manufacturer brand that feature products of only that brand. They hold a larger range of items of that particular brand than other departmental stores. For example, a Nike outlet store will feature more variants of Nike products than a regular departmental store that also features Nike products. Further discounts can be availed at such stores.

Junior Departmental Stores

These are departmental stores that are smaller in size and only feature products of a high price range that cannot be found in regular stores. In these stores the different departments usually operate on their own and have their independent checkout operative. However, it is still owned by a single organization and management.

Category Specific Stores

A good example of such a departmental store would be 'ToysRus', a toy and children product-specific departmental store. Such stores are based on a large category of items such as food and groceries, or baby needs, etc. All products related to that category can be found in the store but no other categories.

Warehouse Stores

These are some of the largest departmental stores that double as warehouse for the various brands. They usually store products in bulk quantities and also sell them in a similar manner. These departmental stores operate in slightly different manners such as providing member-only stores, etc. Costco Wholesale is an example of a warehouse type of departmental store.

DISCOUNT STORE

A **discount store** or **discounter** offers a retail format in which products are sold at prices that are in principle lower than an actual or supposed "full retail price". Discounters rely on bulk purchasing and efficient distribution to keep down costs.

TYPES OF DISCOUNT STORE

Hypermarkets (superstores)

Discount superstores such as Walmart or Target sell general merchandise in a big-box store; many have a full grocery selection and are thus hypermarkets, though that term is not generally used in North America.[2] In the 1960s and 1970s the term "discount department store" was used, and chains such as Kmart, Zodys and TG&Y billed themselves as such.[3] The term "discount department store" or "off-price department store" is sometimes applied to big-box discount retailers of apparel and home goods, such as Ross Dress For Less, Marshalls, and Kohls.

Category killers

So-called category killer stores, specialize in one type of merchandise and sell it in big-box stores. Examples include:

- Apparel: Ross Dress For Less, Marshalls, Kohls, etc.
- Pet supplies: Petco, Petsmart
- Home furnishings and accessories: Big Lots, HomeGoods
- Office supplies: Staples, Office Depot, OfficeMax

Warehouse clubs

When membership is required, discount superstores are known as warehouse clubs, and often require purchases of larger sizes or quantities of goods than a regular superstore. The main national chains, both of which have operations outside the U.S., are Costco and Sam's Club.

Discount grocery store

Major discount grocery store retail chains in the U.S. include Aldi, Lidl, Trader Joe's, Save-A-Lot and Grocery Outlet.[4] Currently Aldi and Lidl are the largest discount retailers in the world operating more than 12,000 discount stores worldwide

CHALLENGES FOR FASHION RETAIL IN INDIA

In the ever-growing globalised world, the Indian textiles and apparel industry is linked to both the Indian and global economy. The Indian economy is one of the fastest growing economies of the world and is witnessing major shifts in consumer preferences. With increasing disposable income, higher living standards, increasing brand consciousness, exposure to trends through media and internet, the Indian fashion industry is positioned to grow at a promising rate.

While many eCommerce businesses have transformed the coronavirus pandemic into an opportunity, some are still struggling to manage their inventory and order fulfillment rates. The state of fashion 2021 report by McKinsey & Company says that businesses need to reduce complexity and find different ways to escalate full-price sell-through to reduce inventory levels by taking a demand-focused approach to their assortment strategy.

Unlike last year, this year, the eCommerce sector per se has not been able to escape from the onslaught of the pandemic. In the recent article by ET Retail, the fashion and accessories sales dipped 22%. However, people have tasted the benefits of online shopping, making their appetites grow continuously in the long run.

The apparel industry has always been persistent to dress up in the changing scenario. Change has always been the wardrobe essential of this industry, happening almost every quarter of each year. According to the 2021 Fashion Report of Unicommerce, the online fashion industry witnessed an order volume growth of 51 % and a gross merchant value (GMV) increase of 45% in FY21 as compared to the previous financial year. With a rotational shift happening in the industry, Unicommerce decided to go ahead and curate eCommerce fashion trends, challenges, opportunities, and solutions that can help you manage and schedule your business action plan . **Trends in the Apparel Industry**

While the demand for athleisure upsurges, there are certain segments that have seen constant growth amid the pandemic. Here are a few trends to watch in 2022 apart from the growing demand for athleisure.

- **Sustainable and Ethical Fashion:** The fashion and clothing industry is often criticized for increasing environmental pollution. With the onset of the coronavirus pandemic and rising issues of climate change, the environmental concerns have gradually increased, making people swear by sustainable clothing materials. Post COVID-19, there has been a rise in the number of people buying high-quality products produced using recycled materials. Some of the fashion brands such as Mio Borsa, Rengé, InSom, Liva, No Nasties are changing the concept of conscious fashion in India.

- **Lingerie and Intimate wear:** As personal hygiene has become a hot topic for both men and women, this segment has also seen a gradual surge in the demand. Moreover, the lockdown is also one of the reasons why the demand for lingerie and innerwear is increasing. Leading lingerie and innerwear brands such as Enamor, Body Care, Amante, Clovis, Jockey, etc. are adapting to advanced technologies to improve their business operations.

- **Readymade clothes:** The major trend of the last few years has not been dipped completely. Trending ready-made fashion brands such as Taavi, Libas, Bhama Couture, Aurelia, W, Indya, etc. have occupied a major part of the online retail space. Right from the women's readymade ethnic Kurtas to men's casual and formal wear, the trend is still here to stay in 2022.

- **Kidswear:** As the coronavirus pandemic is posing a great threat, parents are worried about their kids getting infected, thus avoiding going out and buying clothes from Retail stores. This has caused a huge upsurge in order volume by over 200% order volume growth in 2021. Little Kangaroos, Gini and Jony, Nauti Nati, and Allen Solly Junior are some of the leading brands in Kidswear.

Opportunities in the Apparel Industry

The post-COVID times have supplied great opportunities to the online apparel and fashion industry. Clothes are one of the basic amenities and it wouldn't be wrong to say that this is the only reason why there has been a boom in the purchase of apparel online even during the preventive lockdown. Right from selecting and buying the clothes to returning/exchanging them via online channels, the textile industry is seen to boom at an enormous rate.

E- RETAILING – GROWTH AND DEVELOPMENT

The behavior of customers dictates to retailers how to develop successful new products and gives a great insight (if correctly analysed) into customer shopping habits and behaviour. Historical data has often been a dictator of future trends so it should be no surprise that the creative process in fashion retailing often begins with analysing consumer trend data, sales information and customer feedback from the previous season. Retailers also routinely consult market research reports (such as those written by or) in order to defi ne the competition and further analyse the market and environmental trend factors that are most relevant to their customers. Market research provides an invaluable insight into the industry; the data is combined with other key macro-environmental infl uences (the key drivers affecting both the retailer or business and its customers) to help designers capture the spirit of the times

ONLINE SHOPPING

Online shopping is a form of electronic commerce which allows consumers to directly buy goods or services from a seller over the Internet using a web browser or a mobile app. Consumers find a product of interest by visiting the website of the retailer directly or by searching among alternative vendors using a shopping search engine, which displays the same product's availability and pricing at different e-retailers. As of 2020, customers can shop online using a range of different computers and devices, including desktop computers, laptops, tablet computers and smartphones.

An online shop evokes the physical analogy of buying products or services at a regular "bricks-and-mortar"retailer or shopping center; the process is called business-to-consumer (B2C) online shopping. When an online store is set up to enable businesses to buy from another businesses, the process is called business-to-business (B2B) online shopping. A typical online store enables the customer to browse the firm's range of products and services, view photos or images of the products, along with information about the product specifications, features and prices.

Online stores usually enable shoppers to use "search" features to find specific models, brands or items. Online customers must have access to the Internet and a valid method of payment in order to complete a transaction, such as a credit card, an Interac-enabled debit card, or a service such as PayPal. For physical products (e.g., paperback books or clothes), the e-tailer ships the products to the customer; for digital products, such as digital audio files of songs or software, the e-tailer usually sends the file to the customer over the Internet. The largest of these online retailing corporations are Alibaba, Amazon.com, and eBay

FASHION GOODS ONLINE

Online shopping is a form of electronic commerce which allows consumers to directly buy goods or services from a seller over the Internet using a web browser or a mobile app. ... Online stores usually enable shoppers to use "search" features to find specific models, brands or items.

PRICING

Pricing is one of the most important factors in the field of Trade. Pricing to a commodity means attaching value to the product. To purchase or sell it both the consumer taking the product and the seller giving off the product benefits from the 'value' in return for some bearing. Like the customer gives the money to the seller to take up the 'value' of the product and the seller gives off the product to earn the 'value' of money selling the product.

It is a process in which we decide the value a manufacturer or a seller gets when he offers his goods or services. In this process, both the producer and consumer negate to mutually benefit at an equitably profitable price. It is dependent on various things like how much the company has spent on the inputs, what is the value of a product in the market, what is the need of the product to the customer etc., All the producers and businessmen want to earn profits when they start a business. But, the expected price might vary according to the market conditions, prices of supplementary and complementary goods, changes in input cost like hike in raw materials, labour cost etc.,

Pricing being the basic necessity of trade are discussed further in this section.

What is Price in Marketing?

Price is the amount which one pays for a good or service or any idea. This is the amount for which the product is exchanged with potential customers. Pricing the product or the service is the most essential for a business decision that is to be made by the owner of the business.

One must attach the price to the product which the target market is willing to pay, they should also keep in mind the profit margin they need to acquire to hit their target. This all will help the business to endeavour.

Other approaches are also included in fixing the price of the commodity or service. These approaches include:

- The accountability of cost,
- The degree of competition prevailing,
- The customer's expectation from the product, and so forth.

'Right Price' is one of the important criteria for business success. The right pricing policy is a guideline set by the top-level managers to achieve good sales of the product. Price is indeed a weapon to bring competition in the market, to change the satisfaction level of the consumers. The distribution channel of distribution is affected by the pricing policy.

Both the terms price and 'Pricing' are different in their aspect, Pricing is the method of translating the value of the product in price or quantitative amounts like rupees or dollars.

PRICING POLICIES AND STRATEGIES FOR APPAREL PRODUCTS

The range plan is essential for determining product mix. The plan contains complete detail of all styles, including the required lead times for each style and how many phases are going to exist within each range. The overall styling direction and theme of each range will usually be determined at this stage. Within a season phases are timed for each collection, which allows new colour statements and products to be introduced. The team of designers, buyers and merchandisers will determine the total number of styles required per category of product, such as knitwear or tailoring. They will analyse the proportion and balance of each range, such as quantity of tops versus trousers or daywear versus evening wear (usually there will be more tops than bottoms and more daywear than occasion wear). They will also decide what percentage of each range will be fashion, classic or basics. Finally, they make decisions on types of fabrics and numbers of colours per style, based on trends, availability and suitability. Additionally, the size ranges will be agreed at this stage, such as skirt and trouser lengths for example, or special fi ts such as petite or tall

FUNCTIONS AND FACTORS INFLUENCING PRICING

The main determinants that affect the price are:

- Product Cost.
- The Utility and Demand.
- The extent of Competition in the market.
- Government and Legal Regulations.
- Pricing Objectives.
- Marketing Methods used.

PRICING STRATEGIES FOR NEW PRODUCTS

Price is an essential part of retail strategy. A pricing strategy can help to determine the speed at which a company achieves its marketing objectives. A low price strategy is used to build sales via volume, as used by retailers such as Primark in the UK and Forever 21 and Target in the USA. A higher price strategy is used by companies selling high-quality products, such as luxury brand Louis Vuitton. Whatever the strategy, the price levels should be set in conjunction with the type of fashion product and be appropriate to market position. It is important for retailers to work closely with suppliers and manufacturers in order to establish price and profi t margins – the retail selling price (RSP). This will ensure that objectives are achieved and that all parties involved are satisfi ed: this will, of course, include the customer and the price they are willing to pay, as well as the requirements of the retailer and the supplier. All parties must cover their overheads and make a profi t to retain sustainability in the long term. Most fashion retailers use price promotions, sales and special offers as part of a pricing strategy. These are usually planned in the budget setting process at the start of each season and accounted for by buying and merchandising teams

HIGH PRICE STRATEGY

Luxury brands use a higher price strategy, which is set in conjunction with fashion product type: exclusive, often limited edition, topquality garments. The pricing strategy should be appropriate to the brand's market position

PRICE MATRIX

Different fashion ranges need different price strategies. Products that are referred to as 'opening price point' (OPP) are high in volume and usually low in price. High fashion items, which involve more risk than basic items, will command a higher price and therefore create a wider margin. An important part of the pricing strategy is to determine customers' spending patterns and average spend per range. It is usual for most fashion brands and retailers to use a price matrix within which they segment ranges into 'good, better and best'. This matrix can help fashion retailers to plan a pricing structure across different levels of fashion products on offer.

METHODS OF SETTING PRICES

Pricing method leads to a specific price. There are various methods used for setting price of the product. Some methods are cost-oriented while some are market-oriented. Each of the methods has its plus and minus points, and applicability. Marketing managers apply the appropriate method for setting the price. The appropriate method can be decided on the basis of the study and analysis of internal and external aspects as well as suitability of the method. Following part describes some widely used pricing methods. See Figure 3.

1. Mark-up Pricing Method:

This is the most commonly used method. The method is also known as cost-plus pricing. In this method, a standard mark-up (or profit margin) is added to the product costs. This method is used in construction business, professions, and even for consumer goods. The method can be used only when company has necessary data about various costs and expected sales. Company may prefer fixed per cent of costs or fixed per cent of selling price.

XYZ Company Limited expects annual sales of 100000 units.

Variable cost per unit is Rs. 10.

Fixed cost is Rs. 500000.

Company wishes to earn 20 % mark-up on selling price, or 25% mark-up on costs.

Cost per unit = variable costs + (Fixed costs/ Unit sales)

= Rs. 10 + Rs. 500000/100000

= Rs. 15

Now, company wants 20% mark-up on selling price,

Naturally, when cost is taken as a base, the rate should be high, as indicated in the example. Company may follow either of approaches, but must know the difference.

Merits:

Keeping in mind a lot of forces affecting market, the mark-up rate may be kept high or low, fixed or variable.

This method is widely used. It offers following merits:

i. It recovers costs as rapidly as possible.

ii. It is relatively a simple method to practice.

iii. If it is used by the entire industry, price tends to be similar. And, price competition can be minimized:'

iv. Experts believe that cost-plus pricing method is fair for both – buyers and sellers.

2. Perceived-value pricing Method:

Perceived-value pricing is a market-oriented method for setting the price. Here, price is based on the consumers' perceived value of the product. Consumers' views on price are given priority. Company takes consumers' perception of value as a key to set the price, and not its own cost and objectives.

Company tries to measure the views of buyers regarding price of the product. Manager explains the consumers about total offers, including core product (key benefits and features), product-related aspects (like brand image, reputation, novelty, etc.), and product- related services (such as after-sales services like free installation, free home delivery, guarantee, etc.) and asks them to estimate price for that product or for total benefits offered by the product.

The key to the perceived-value pricing method is to measure accurately the market's perception of the offer's value. The seller with inflated views of his offers will overprice the product while with underestimated views will charge less than what it should be. Market research is needed to estimate market perception of price. Let us take an example,

ABC Company Limited wants to set price for the motorbike by the perceived-value method. Market research officer considers following aspects and takes the views of buyers.

Buyers respond as under:

Rs. 30000 if the bike is similar to competitors' motorbikes

Rs. 2000 is the price premium for novelty, shape, new getup, and colour.

Rs. 3000 is price premium for the highest mileage per litre petrol.

Rs. 2000 is price premium for replacement guarantee and two extra free services.

Rs. 2000 is price premium for durability and reliability.

Rs. 1000 is price premium for special safety measures.

Merits:

This method offers following merits:

i. Perceived-value method matches with consumer orientation.

ii. It considers indirectly competitors' offers.

iii. It is more realistic than any other method.

iv. Perceived-value can be taken as base, with little adjustment in costs and objectives, the most suitable price can be set.

3. Going-rate Pricing Method:

This is also said as competitive parity method. Even, sometimes, it is called as competition- oriented pricing. The method is, normally, followed by small firms, said as 'the followers' In going- rate pricing method, the company gives less attention to its own costs, objectives, or product demand. But, pricing decision is largely based on competitors' prices.

The company may charge the same, more, or less than major competitors. The notion is "follow the leader," or "leader is right." One must note that company doesn't select a price, which is far below or much higher than the real. However, competitors' pricing is taken as a base. And, final price may be set slight high or low depending upon objectives, qualities of product, and services offered.

Merits:

The method can be justified on the following grounds:

i. It is the only way to set the price when costs are difficult to measure and competitors' response is uncertain.

ii. It considers competitors pricing policies as a base. In contemporary marketing practices, it is more relevant method.

iii. Going rate pricing brings uniform pricing in the industry. It ensures fair return to sellers and harmony in industry.

iv. It may protect consumers' from cheating and misguiding. They can buy the similar product at a, more or less, same price.

4. Sealed-bid Pricing Method:

Sealed-bid pricing is followed in construction or contract business. It is also a competitive pricing method. Here, price is selected on the basis of sealed bids (quotation or estimated price) for the jobs.

The firm sets its price on expectations of how competitors will price the product. The firm wants to win the contract requires submitting the lower price than competitors. However, costs and profits are not totally ignored. The firm cannot set price below the costs.

It is called as tender pricing also. In response to the proposal of jobs or works, interested parties (businessmen or marketers) have to fill the tender (send quotation or estimated costs) stating price and conditions of work and send in forms of sealed-bids.

The bid is an offer of price for particular work or product. Generally sealed-bids (sealed envelops containing a bid) are invited for a competitive work. Offers or proposals come from charitable trusts, companies, organisations, or governments. In our country, we say this method as "tender," and proposal of jobs as a "tender notice."

Mostly, the tender notice is published in newspapers or circulars. The offer or proposal for work contains type of work or job, time to complete the work, quality of work, and other similar conditions.

In response to the tender or proposal, interested parties have to send sealed-bids stating their prices and conditions within the permitted time. In this method, the party inviting the sealed-bids is customer and those who bid by sealed quotations are the marketers (because they will serve the inviting party).

On a due date – either publicly or otherwise – the sealed-bids (or quotations) are opened, and the bid with lower price and more favourable conditions is selected. Rate of selected bid is the price for the job. The selected bid is given the business. The method has its plus and minus points.

5. Target Return Pricing:

This is one of the cost-oriented methods for setting price of the product. Here, the firm determines that level of price at which it can yield the target return on investment. Here, return on investment is taken as a base for price determination.

Attempts are made to recover the cost of investment. Mostly, government Companies, public utilities, cooperative societies, and the similar organisations fix pricing for their products on this basis to ensure minimum return on investment.

For example, Jai Hind Private Limited company expects to sell 10000 school bags of premium quality in the current year. Fixed costs allocated to this line is Rs. 5, 00000. Variable costs estimated for each bag is Rs. 100. Total investment (covering development, production and marketing) on this line is Rs. 50, 00000. Company wants 20% return on investment.

Return on Investment (ROI) = Rs. 5000000 x 20% = Rs. 1000000

Costs per unit = variable cost per unit + fixed cost per unit

= Rs. 100 + (Rs. 500000 ÷ 10000 units)

= Rs. 100 + Rs. 50

= Rs. 150.

Target return (profit) per unit = Rs. 1000000 + 10000 units = Rs. 100.

Selling price per unit = cost of product + Return on Investment.

= Rs. 150 + 100

= Rs. 250.

6. Break-even Analysis Method:

Some companies set the price for their products by Break-Even Analysis (BEP method). It is a managerial tool that establishes relationship among costs, volume of sales, and profits. It is also known as cost-volume-profit analysis.

It involves developing tables and/or charts that help a company to determine at what level of sales, the revenue will be equal to the total costs. Under this method, attempts are made to find out volume of sales at which total costs are just equal to the sales revenue. This is such a level of sales at which there is no profit, no loss.

Sales Revenue = Total Costs.

This level is called BEP (break-even point), at which the firm has neither profits nor losses. The firm just covers its total costs. When sales revenue exceeds the total costs, the result is profit; and when sales revenue is less than total costs, the result is loss. Thus, BEP is the position of sales at which sales revenue is just equal to total costs. BEP can be calculated either by a formula or by a chart.

Formula Method:

BEP can be calculated using formula as under:

For example,

Hindustan Products Pvt. Ltd. gives following details:

Selling price is = Rs. 200 per unit.

Variable cost is = Rs. 100 per unit.

Fixed cost is = Rs. 500000.

Contribution is = selling price – variable costs

= (Rs. 200 – Rs. 100) = Rs. 100

CHAPTER V

SUSTAINABLE FASHION

INTRODUCTION

Sustainable fashion (also known as eco-fashion) is a movement and process of fostering change to fashion products and the fashion system towards greater ecological integrity and social justice. Sustainable fashion concerns more than just addressing fashion textiles or products. It addresses the entire manner in which clothing is produced, who produces it, and how long the life span of a product is before it reaches the landfill. This sustainable movement combats the large carbon footprint that the fashion industry and fast fashion have created by reducing greenhouse gas emissions.Reducing the environmental impact of fashion can combat air pollution, water pollution and overall climate change that could possibly prevent millions of premature deaths over the next century.

Sustainable fashion deals with considering fashion from the perspective of a variety of stakeholders ranging from contemporary producers and consumers of clothes, to future producers and consumers.

In 2020, it was found that an approach of voluntarily self-directed reform of textile manufacturingsupply chains to substantially reduce the environmental impact of fashion by large companies themselves has failed. Measures to reform fashion towards sustainability beyond marketing campaigns of greenwashing may need to involve policies for the creation and enforcement of standardized certificates along with related import control and subsidy and eco-tariffs-like interventions

SUSTAINABLE FASHION - MEANING AND SIGNIFICANCE

Sustainable fashion movement believe that the fashion industry has a clear opportunity to act differently, pursuing profit and growth while also creating new value and deeper wealth for society and therefore for the world economy. They believe that clothing companies ought to place environmental, social, and ethical improvements on management's agenda.The goal of sustainable fashion is to create flourishing ecosystems and communities through its activity. This may include: increasing the value of local production and products; prolonging the lifecycle of materials; increasing the value of timeless garments; reducing the amount of waste; and reducing the harm to the environment created as a result of production and consumption. Another of its aims can sometimes be seen to educate people to practice environmentally friendly consumption by promoting the "green consumer", which can allow for the company itself to gain more support and a larger following.

There are doubts within the movement as to the effectiveness of "green consumerism." Business models based on selling more units of clothing or accessories are widely not considered to be sustainable, regardless of how "eco-friendly" the garments themselves are. Thus the industry has to change its basic premise for profit, yet this is slow coming as it requires a large shift in business practices, models and tools for assessment.This became apparent in the discussions following the Burberry report of the brand burning unsold goods worth around £28.6m (about $37.8 million) in 2018, exposing not only overproduction and subsequent destruction of unsold stock as a normal business practice, but the behavior amongst brands that actively undermine a sustainable fashion agenda.

The challenge for making fashion more sustainable requires to rethink the whole system, and this call for action is in itself not new. The Union of Concerned Researchers in Fashion has argued that the industry is still discussing the same ideas as were originally mooted in the late 1980s and early 1990s. When taking the long view and examining fashion and sustainability progress since the 1990s, there are few actual advances in ecological terms. As the Union observes, "So far, the mission of sustainable fashion has been an utter failure and all small and incremental changes have been drowned by an explosive economy of extraction, consumption, waste and continuous labor abuse."

A frequently asked question of those working in the area of sustainable fashion is whether the field itself is an oxymoron. This reflects the seemingly irreconcilable possibility of bringing together fashion (understood as constant change, and tied to business models based on continuous replacement of goods) and sustainability (understood as continuity and resourcefulness).The apparent paradox dissolves if fashion is seen more broadly, not only as a process aligned to expansionist business models, and consumption of new clothing, but instead as mechanism that leads to more engaged ways of livingon a precious and changing earth.

ENVIRONMENTAL CONCERNS RELATED TO FASHION

The fashion industry is one of the major polluting industries in the world. The industry produces an estimated 10% of all greenhouse gas emissions.The production and distribution of the crops, fibers, and garments used in fashion all contribute to differing forms of environmental pollution, including water, air, and soil pollution.The textile industry is the second greatest polluter of local freshwater in the world, and is culpable for roughly one-fifth of all industrial water pollution.Some of the main factors that contribute to this industrial caused pollution are the vast overproduction of fashion items,the use of synthetic fibers, and the agriculture pollution of fashion crops.

LINEAR FASHION

A linear medium is any medium which is intended to be written to or accessed in a linear fashion, literally meaning in a line. A book containing an encyclopedia however is a non-linear medium, as it is not necessary for the articles to be accessed (or written) in any particular order.

A linear process or development is one in which something changes or progresses straight from one stage to another, and has a starting point and an ending point.

CIRCULAR FASHION

A number of emerging business models go under the name of "circular fashion," inspired by the circular economy. While there are many models under development, some are gaining more traction.Much of the work on circular fashion builds on ideas and initiatives explored in the 1990s and onwards, by scholars such as Lynda Grose, Kate Fletcher, Rebecca Earley, Mathilda Tham and Timo Rissanen, especially the thinking around the "metabolism" of garments and wardrobes, "zero waste" production, and the focus on the whole life cycle of garments. The popular terminology around circular fashion, reached the mainstream through a report that has come to define the field, the 2017 "A New Textile Economy: Redesigning Fashion's Future" by the Ellen MacArthur foundation.

SUSTAINABILITY

- Repair
- Recycle
- Reuse and reduce.

One model suggests a perspective emphasizing the "Power of Nature" which is the industry looking into materials that have always been looked at as waste as a more sustainable method to making new clothing.[118] The materials that will mitigate negative impacts from the industry include vegan materials from the earth and recycling old fabric into new clothing.

Rental and sharing models

Another models is based on "Rent a Closet"; this initiative has been around for a while. This trend ultimately lowers the new purchase of clothing and disposal of clothing, which means less waste. Rent is a company building on the "Rent a Closet" approach to consumption, where a consumer leases a garment instead of purchasing it. Rent the Runway started as a company that would rent out luxury items to people who may not be able to afford the clothing at regular retail price. Renting and sharing clothing is also known as CFC (collaborative fashion consumption) a sustainable fashion trend consumers are getting involved in.

Vintage and resale models

Another trend is the revival and recirculation of vintage clothing.Vintage clothing is a way to lower the amount of clothing that gets disposed of and ends up in landfills. Companies like SHEKOU Vintage, RE/DONE, Vintage Twin and Frankie Collective sell repaired vintage clothing. Repairing and reselling clothing has less negative impact than creating new clothing does.

Rethinking recycling

A more technologically-minded trend is "innovative recycling", which seeks to view waste itself as a source of value. Within the fashion industry, some manufacturers have created incentives for consumers to participate in the recycling of their clothing. Innovative recycling is also aimed at clothing stores themselves, who do not always have sustainable methods to properly dispose of boxes and plastic bags; innovative recycling also looks at the packaging that clothes come in having been sent from manufacturers. A change in approaches towards recycling within the fashion industry could potentially greatly impact the amount of waste the industry creates.

From collective to connective

Using digital technologies and blockchain can promote more "Connected Clothes" which allows for more opportunities in digitalizing clothing for personalization, life-tracking, and traceability of its origin.

Tailored resurgence

Tailored couture is argued could be one option for the future of a greener fashion industry, for those who can afford it, as it can potentially lead to less waste and more jobs improving the economy. Tailored couture is no longer desired because of the convenience of malls and stores provide but the consequence of the convenience is the pollution of the environment. The idea is that tailored clothing can reduce mass-production, while reusing and redesigning old clothes to fit could reduce the amount of old worn out unfitting clothes thrown out or given away

SUSTAINABLE FASHION - ECO FASHION

The fashion industry has a disastrous impact on the environment. In fact, it is the second largest polluter in the world, just after the oil industry. And, the environmental damage is increasing as the industry grows.

The textiles and fashion industries are amongst the leading industries that affect the environment negatively. One of the industries that greatly jeopardize environmental sustainability is the textiles and fashion industry, which thus also bears great responsibilities. Globalization has made it possible to produce clothing at increasingly lower prices, prices so low, and collections shifting so fast, that many consumers consider fashion to be disposable.However, fast, and thus disposable, fashion adds to pollution and generates environmental hazards, in production, use, and disposal.

Putting the environmental perspective at the center, rather than the logic of the industry, is thus an urgent concern if fashion is to become more sustainable. The Earth Logic fashion research action plan argues for "putting the health and survival of our planet earth and consequently the future security and health of all species including humans, before industry, business, and economic growth."In making this argument the Earth Logic plan explicitly connects the global fashion system with the 2018 IPCC Special Report on Global Warming of 1.5 °C.

Furthermore, the Earth Logic fashion research action plan sets out a range of possible areas for work in a sustainable fashion that scientific and research evidence suggests are the most likely to deliver a change of the scale and pace needed to respond to challenges like climate change. Earth Logic's point of departure is that the planet, and its people, must be put first, before profit. It replaces the logic of economic growth, which is arguably the single largest factor limiting change towards sustainable fashion, with the logic that puts earth at its center.

SLOW FASHION

Slow fashion can be seen as an alternative approach against fast fashion, based on principles of the slow food movement.Characteristics of sustainable fashion match the philosophies of "slow fashion" in that emotional, ecological and ethical qualities are favored over uniform and bland convenience with minimal friction. It requires a changed infrastructure and a reduced through-put of goods. Categorically, slow fashion is neither business-as-usual nor just involving design classics. Nor is it production-as-usual but with long lead times. Slow fashion is a vision of the fashion sector built from a different starting point. Slow fashion is a fashion concept that reflects a perspective, which respects human living conditions, biological, cultural diversity and scarce global resources and creates unique, personalized products.

The term Slow Fashion came about quite organically. It was coined by Kate Fletcher of the Centre for Sustainable Fashion, following the phenomena of the slow food movement.As with the slow food movement, Fletcher saw a need for a slower pace in the fashion industry.

Slow fashion challenges growth fashion's obsession with mass-production and globalized style. It becomes a guardian of diversity and changes the power relations between fashion creators and consumers, therefore forging new relationships and trust that are only possible at smaller scales. It fosters a heightened state of awareness of the design process and its impacts on resource flows, workers, communities, and ecosystems.

Slow fashion often consists of durable products, traditional production techniques, or design concepts that strive to be season-less or last aesthetically and materially for longer periods of time. The impact of slowness aims to affect many points of the production chain. For workers in the textile industry in developing countries, slow fashion means higher wages. For end-users, slow fashion means that the goods are designed and manufactured with greater care and high-quality products. From an environmental point of view, it means that there are less clothing and industrial waste that is removed from use following transient trends.Emphasis is put on durability; emotionally, materially, aesthetically, and/or through services that prolong the use-life of garments. New ideas and product innovations are constantly redefining slow fashion, so using a static, single definition would ignore the evolving nature of the concept.

Examples of stability of expression over long times are abundant in the history of dress, not least in ethnic or folk dress, ritual or coronation robes, clerical dress, or the uniforms of the Vatican Guard.The emphasis on slowness in branding is thus an approach that is specific for a niche in the market (such as Western-educated middle-class) that has since the 1990s become dominated by "fast" models. One of the earliest brands that gained global fame with an explicit focus on slow fashion, the Anglo-Japanese brand People Tree, embraces the concept of ethical trade, manufactures all products in accordance with ethical commerce standards, and supports local producers and craftsmen in developing countries. The People Tree brand is known as the first fashion to receive the World Fair Trade Organization product label in 2013, demonstrating their dedication to fair trade and the environment.In addition to adopting ethical trade, the brand also prefers to use nature-friendly materials, textile products with GOTS certification and local, natural, recyclable material.

The concept of slow fashion is however not without its controversies, as the imperative of slowness is a mandate emerging from a position of privilege. To stop consuming "fast fashion" strikes against low-income consumers whose only means to access trends is through cheap and accessible goods. Those who are already having a high position in society can afford to slow down and cement their status and position, while those on their way up resent being told to stay at the lower rungs of the status hierarchy "The prestige of slowness allows a cultural signifier for those already have social positions to preserve, and have time and money to take it easy and enjoy the pleasures of reflection and meditate over their moral superiority."

Another obstacle that the "slow fashion" paradigm is facing is related to consumers' behavior towards the consumption of fashion and specifically clothing. In fact, sustainability-conscious consumers, that usually take into account the social and environmental implications of their purchases, may experience an attitude-behavior gap preventing them to change their consumption habits when it comes to choosing ethical clothing. Purchasing fashion is still perceived as an action connected to social status and it is still strongly emotionally driven.

ENVIRONMENTAL IMPACT OF FAST FASHION INSPECTION

One of the most apparent reasons for the current unsustainable condition of the fashion system is related to the temporal aspects of fashion; the continuous stream of new goods onto the market, or what is popularly called "fast fashion." The term has come to signify cheap, accessible, and on-trend clothes sourced through global production chains and sold through chains such as H&M, Zara, Forever21, etc. A popular fast-fashion retailer called Shein which is most notably advertised on social media platform Tiktok, is one of the most visited fast-fashion websites in the world and ships to 220 countries, however, many people have begun to question how ethical and sustainable Shein is as it is responsible for about 706 billion kilograms of greenhouse gases in 2015 from the production of polyester textiles and makes up for hundreds of gallons of water being used for one garment.The fashion industry has a value of three trillion dollars. It is two percent of the world's gross domestic product (GDP) - the total monetary or market value of all the finished goods and services produced within a country's borders in a specific time period.Out of the three trillion dollars, the majority is made of fast fashion.

However, the "fast" aspect of consumption is primarily a problem for the environment when done on a massive scale. As long as fast conspicuous consumption was reserved to the rich, the global impact was not reaching public attention or seen as a problem. That is, "fast" shopping sprees of haute couture is not seen as a problem, rather it is celebrated (for example in movies such as Pretty Woman), whereas when people with less means shop fast fashion it is seen as unethical and a problem. Today, the speed of fast fashion is common across the whole industry as exclusive fashion replicates the fast fashion chains with continuous releases of collections and product drops: the quality of a garment does not necessarily translate to a slower pace of consumption and waste.These releases are only exasperated by the acceleration of fashion trends. As micro-trends are only lasting an average of 3 years, the demand for clothes has also accelerated.

Fast fashion has negative effects on the environment and is unethical in terms of production. In order to make clothing fast enough to keep up with the changing fashion trends, the clothes are produced in harmful ways. "Fast" clothing is made with synthetic fibers as opposed to natural fibers. The synthetic fibers are made using the Earth's fossil fuels. Almost sixty percent of our clothes are made this way. Since people spend so much money on these types of clothes and purchase them so frequently, landfills are filling up quickly. Over sixty percent of clothes made every year end up in landfills as consumer waste, and almost twenty percent of the world's waste is constituted by fashion products. Production of these types of clothing is also commonly exploitative, with most factories that produce "fast" clothing employing workers on low wages in exploitative environments. Exploitative fast fashion production is prevalent in countries like China, Bangladesh and Vietnam. Hard labour was always around in the fashion industry dating back to when slave labour helped factories gather their materials. People making these clothes today suffer from harsh working conditions, low wages, and risks to health and safety.

9 798887 337517

Printed by Libri Plureos GmbH in Hamburg,
Germany